A COMPLETE HANDS

RENDEZVOUS
WITH
PRACTICAL SOLIDITY

SOLIDITY FOR NOVICE PROFESSIONALS,
ADVANCED PROGRAMMERS, ARCHITECTS,
STUDENTS AND ACADEMICIANS

HARISH JAGGI | RAJ JHA

INDIA • SINGAPORE • MALAYSIA

Notion Press

Old No. 38, New No. 6
McNichols Road, Chetpet
Chennai - 600 031

First Published by Notion Press 2019
Copyright © Harish Jaggi & Raj Jha 2019
All Rights Reserved.

ISBN 978-1-64760-661-9

Contents

Acknowledgments

Harish Jaggi

First and foremost I would like to thank almighty God and my spiritual guide Dr. Avdhoot Shivanand. Writing book is an arduous ordeal and a long journey. You instilled strength and power in me to believe in the dream of writing something unique. This would not have been possible without Shiv-Shiva and my guru. First attitude of gratitude is towards you for anything I accomplish.

To my mother and father, Dr. Saroj Jaggi and Dr. Vijay Jaggi: I have no words to express thanks for all the wisdom, love and support you've given me. All my accomplishments are a result of your blessings. My heartfelt regards to my father-in-law [Mr. Ramesh Sikka] and mother-in-law [Mrs. Shashi Sikka] for your affection and unconditional support.

To my wife, Dr. Vaishali Jaggi: I am so grateful to have you as my life partner. Thank you for the unconditional sacrifice you made in last one year as I did burn lot of midnight oil in completing this book. Thanks for not just believing, but having full conviction that I could pull this through

To my kids, Aryan and Ayush: You are the best gift I have ever received. You get me going. This book is a small legacy that both you gems need to emulate and take a big leap in driving excellence.

To my brother, Vineet Jaggi and family [Dr. Shikha, Aarna, Aadya]: You are an invaluable pillar of support. Thank you for your best wishes at every juncture. Aarna: We have a reason to visit Frank Pepe!

A big thanks to my friend Raj for being a genius mind. Research done by you on several topics is exemplary that brings essence of learning strait and clear.

Last but not the least – Tons of thanks to the great minds behind genesis of revolutionary Blockchain technology, its proponents and our readers. Hope this book turns out to be an enriching experience to all Blockchain enthusiasts.

Raj Jha

Writing a book is harder than I thought and more rewarding than I could have ever imagined. None of this would have been possible without my wife Shailaza, she stood by me during every struggle and all my successes. I greatly value her contribution and deeply appreciate her belief in me. I appreciate my baby, my little girl Ahana for abiding my ignorance and the patience she showed during my book writing. Words would never say how grateful I am to both of you. I consider myself the luckiest in the world to have such a lovely and caring family, standing beside me with their love and unconditional support.

I owe thanks to my brother Ajay and family [Payal, Abhinav] and sister Reena and family [Deepak, Shreya, Tushar] for their selfless love and care. My heartfelt regard goes to my father in law, mother in law for their love and moral support.

I thank the Almighty for giving me the strength and patience to work through all these years so that today I can stand proudly with my head held high.

I am extremely thankful to my dear friend Harish for his exceptional help and guidance in making this book so engaging for readers.

Finally, I would like to dedicate this work to my late father who taught me to be an independent and determined person, to my late mother without whom I would never be able to achieve my objectives and succeed in life.

Harish and Raj

Special thanks to our guide and mentor, Sajal Singhal who is a renowned Blockchain speaker. We are indeed privileged to have you around, and inspiring us to dream big and aim high. You are indeed an institution.

A big thanks to our friends Rajneesh, Ruchin and Raveena for your valuable suggestions in making this book a delightful treat.

CHAPTER 1

Solidity Rendezvous

Disclaimer: This is a complete hands on book. Copy code recipes in each chapter on Remix or your local VScode setup to infer and analyze results of each example. Comments are added in each recipe to guide readers from all walks of life - It is recommended not to overlook comments. Steps to use Remix or your local VScode environment are explained in the book. We strongly recommend to play with the code recipes to reap complete benefits and attain practical expertise on Solidity. We tried hard to rectify formatting of code recipes after porting them from editor to this book but due to definitive size of book pages, it is not ideal despite all efforts. We recommend readers to copy and paste code recipes in your own environment to view recipes with correct and ideal formatting. All the best.

Introduction to Smart Contracts

Smart contracts genesis might look very recent; concept however was incepted way back in 1996 when Nick Szabo coined this term referring to "a set of promises specified in digital form that encompasses protocols to be used by parties to fulfill these promises". According to him, smart contracts shall improve execution of the four basic contract design objectives namely observability, verifiability, privacy and enforceability.

If we breakdown szabo's vision and map it to current smart contract framework then we can easily conclude that, his definition is still relevant and captures the essence of smart contracts. See his mapping with current ethereum smart contract framework – You will concur with our inference.

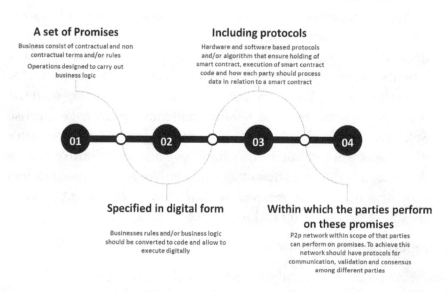

Smart contract is a self-executable, self-enforceable, and self-verifiable computer program that runs on certain decentralized environment (For example blockchain). The purpose of smart contract is to execute contract or provisions of contract between transacting parties (example suppliers and buyers) by taking custody over any transferable digital assets along with unambiguous instructions for transfer of assets to the ledger.

Smart contract can be triggered only through the events (transactions) and can eventually cascade into more events. Once an event triggers the terms of the contract, the corresponding code is automatically executed.

Every single flow of the program is driven by the events. Smart contract maintains state and with every transaction or event, the state of smart contract changes. Actually smart contract variables use blockchain storage and every change in variable value triggers change in the state of blockchain. For example - If you transfer $500 from one account to second using smart contract then it will change state for both the account values saved on blockchain. This is the real essence behind the concept.

In 2009, Bitcoin blockchain emerged with very limited form of rudimentary smart contracts. Bitcoin smart contracts could not satisfy all propositions suggested by Szabo due to its complications to code business rules with its low-level programming language i.e. 'Bitcoin Script'. Bitcoin Script language functionality is not as programmable and extensible as solidity on ethereum. Bitcoin script language hence does not qualify as 'Turing Complete Language' especially for not supporting loops. Programmers however can simulate any loop by repeating underlying code many a times with the help of if statements. An imperative language is 'Turing Complete' if it has conditional and loop (such as if, while, loop, break, for etc.) statements in built along with ability to maintain arbitrary number of variables.

In 2015, Ethereum presented enhanced ability to build complex smart contracts by propagating smart contract language named 'Solidity'. Solidity is 'Turing Complete' language and it enables developers to write complex contracts in a short span of time with less verbose code. Impactful ethereum protocols along with flexible solidity language led to the resurrection of smart contract theme thereby increasing its popularity in enhancing efficiencies of business contracts. Solidity integrates Szabo's original idea into new age blockchain technology however overall theme probably proved way more difficult than it was initially conceptualized. Reason as we understand is – Writing solidity code is easier however securing and scaling it is cumbersome and challenging.

Vitalik Buterin, Ethereum's initiator, designed Ethereum with smart contracts in such a way that anyone can create smart contracts using Ethereum Virtual Machine (EVM). EVM is a programming environment for executing solidity code on blockchain. EVM is distributed global computer where all smart contracts are executed thus ethereum is sometimes referred to as a "world computer" where smart contracts live in the form of bytecode within the decentralized database on all nodes.

Legislatively smart contract is defined as "an event-driven program that maintains state, and runs on distributed, decentralized, shared and replicated ledger that executes contract or its provision(s) by taking custody and instructing transfer of assets on the ledger".

Let's ponder over events and assets to get complete background.

Event – We can never repeat an event because of unique time dimension associated with every event. Ideally events are immutable because we cannot modify them through any means or actions. Any future modifications to already occurred events require the advent of new and different events (which may or may not undo the impact of original event). This is the concept that blockchain brings on the foray i.e. events are transactions and transactions are immutable. Even smart contracts are permanent and absolute hence are different from traditional software code or application. Immutability of smart contracts enhance trust among contracting parties – this is the most prominent feature of blockchain.

Event-Driven Program - Smart contract can get triggered by events (transactions) and reciprocally they can trigger events. Once an event triggers pertinent terms of the contract, relevant code automatically gets executed. Entire flow of contracts is determined and governed by events.

Assets – Blockchain assets are type of digital assets having representation in cryptocurrency.

Now let us understand legislative definition with a real-world example:

Imagine a blockchain based decentralized auction platform on ethereum; which has unique set of rules for managing auctions. On this platform, sellers can create assets and auction them. Once a famous painter (seller) decided to use this platform to sell one of his premium paintings. Painter didn't analyze the painting value beforehand however intended to reap highest bid from potential buyers. He formulated arbitrary base value for the painting so that buyers bid more than this stipulation. Auction platform has multiple deployed smart contracts for managing auction and there are multiple terms of contract coded into smart contracts. Application has following functionalities:

1. Anonymous users can bid

2. Bidders should submit identity details along with bid quote

3. Bidders bid for asset and contract withholds bid amount in ETH

4. Bidders cannot bid value lesser than base value

5. Seller can create digital asset for the painting

6. Seller transfers ownership of asset to the auction contract and thereafter activates auction

7. Smart contract holds custody of digital asset until terms of contracts are not fulfilled

8. Time of auction is 24 hours

9. Bidder with highest bid will be declared winner

10. If there are multiple highest bids, then bidder with lowest timestamp will win

11. Smart contract will publish an event notifying winner to pay amount from his wallet

12. Winner will initiate new transaction to pay currency via smart contract

13. Smart contract will transfer currency from winner's wallet to painter's wallet

14. Smart contract will then transfer ownership from painter to winner

15. At the end, closure of bid takes place by sending congratulation note to both painter and winner

As you can see, smart contract has played multiple roles to qualify legislative definition. Below are prominent actions:

1. Creation of digital asset and assignment of ownership basis business logic

2. Custody of digital asset until all contract terms are satisfied and winner settles due payment

3. Record and store data in ledger through transactions

4. Compare values to determine highest bid using credible algorithm

5. Track changes in state over time until closure

6. Validate various contract terms and conditions

7. Publish event to interact with DApp

8. Accept wallet payment

9. Transfer ownership

10. Maintain all states in ledger and do audit trail

If we visualize high-level model of smart contracts, then it will look like below depiction:

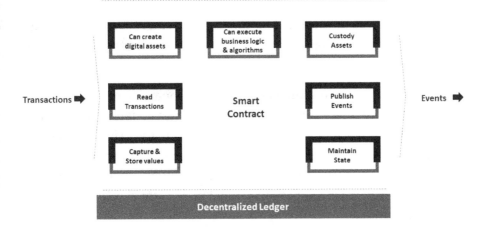

Smart contract we visualized above was deterministic because clauses we embed are a form of conditional logic i.e. On occurrence of a specified event and/or at a specified time, a deterministic action is required to take place. Let us add one new condition/clause in our smart contract logic to make our contract non-deterministic.

The winner of contract should not have any criminal background.

With this new contract clause, our smart contract will become non-deterministic, since to decide winner, smart contract now needs to retrieve information from third party government agencies to ascertain criminal background of winner. Here oracles come into picture, due to security reasons smart contract languages including solidity are purely deterministic and they cannot fetch information from sources outside blockchain boundary. Smart contracts need to be deterministic because each nodes of the network must find same result given the same input for a particular contract method. If this proposition becomes non-affirmative, then each node that executes the contract method to validate the transaction may end up producing different results and hence no consensus would ever be possible. We will discuss working of oracles in depth including the mechanism it follows to allow smart contracts to fetch data outside blockchain network.

Having attained sufficient knowledge of smart contract and its overall operating methodology, let's deep-dive on solidity programming language.

Solidity word means quality or state of being firm or strong in structure. Solidity is firm because it is always deterministic and permanent. It demands developer's mindset to drive embedded firmware (thermostat, microwave) development rather just traditional software development. In firmware development, it is difficult to update or fix bugs. Developers has to get code right the first time that requires discipline.

Understand Solidity Programming Language

Gavin Wood and team (Yoichi Hirai, Christian Reitwiessner, and Alex Beregszaszi) developed solidity language to allow developers to write ethereum contracts with less efforts and high precision. Solidity syntax is based on JavaScript and many of its concepts are harvested from python and C++. As we stated before, solidity is an easy language to code but difficult to secure and scale as it is public (code is always publicly available) and open (can call other contracts and even call self to max stack depth 1024). Let us cruise through prominent properties of solidity language. We will use these features throughout the example recipes in this book so be watchful to make a solid beginning.

Solidity uses 'design by contract' or 'contract-oriented' approach to verify execution of methods and to ensure that state of data structures and overall contract do not get corrupted. Bertrand Meyer coined term "design by contract" in 1986 while working on Eiffel programing language. It allows developers to define formal elements such as pre-conditions, post-conditions and invariants for every contract method to guarantee valid execution of contract.

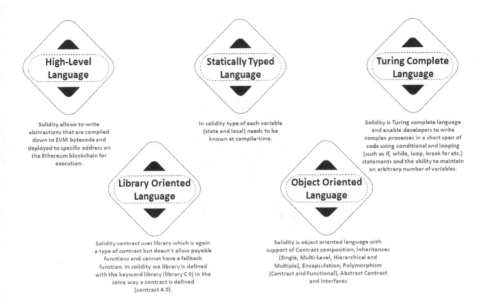

High-Level Language

Solidity allows to write abstractions that are compiled down to EVM bytecode and deployed to specific address on the Ethereum blockchain for execution.

Statically Typed Language

In solidity type of each variable (state and local) needs to be known at compile-time.

Turing Complete Language

Solidity is Turing complete language and enable developers to write complex processes in a short span of code using conditional and looping (such as if, while, loop, break for etc.) statements and the ability to maintain an arbitrary number of variables.

Library Oriented Language

Solidity contract uses library which is again a type of contract but doesn't allow payable functions and cannot have a fallback function. In solidity we library is defined with the keyword library (library C 0) in the same way a contract is defined (contract A 0).

Object Oriented Language

Solidity is object oriented language with support of Contract composition, Inheritances (Single, Multi-Level, Hierarchical and Multiple), Encapsulation, Polymorphism (Contract and Functional), Abstract Contract and Interfaces

In contract-oriented approach, an automatic contract (relation) is established between program (supplier) and program users (consumers). 'Contract' in this context is actually not a smart contract but contractual relation between supplier and consumer. Consumers can be app, system, program, class, or contract. For example - If smart contract 'Tech' is using smart contract 'Solution' then 'Tech is Consumer' and 'Solution is Supplier'. Contract (relation) gets established between them automatically. 'Tech' can use functions of 'Solution' only when pre, invariant and post conditions are satisfied. Contract 'Solution' can also become consumer and consume functions of any other supplier contract based on its association. Every smart contract and its functions should abide 'design by contract' approach by design.

Pre-conditions – Statements that are true before a contract function call. The supplier warrants its demand from consumer.

Post-conditions – Statements that must be true after the function execution is complete. The supplier promises it to consumer.

Invariants – Statements that are always true before and after contract function call and never change.

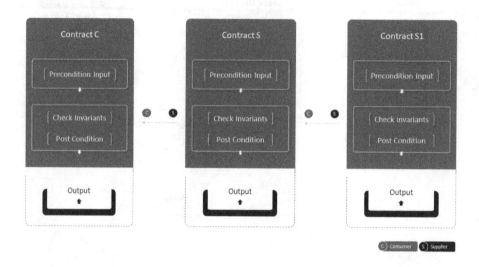

Getting Ready to Explore Solidity
Pre Deep Dive Considerations

- Install visual studio code for Windows/Linux/Mac from https://code.visualstudio.com/

- Install Solidity visual studio code extension from visual studio market place - https://marketplace.visualstudio.com/items?itemName=JuanBlanco.solidity

- Install extension for material icon theme

- Go to https://code.visualstudio.com/ and download visual studio code for Windows/Linux/Mac.

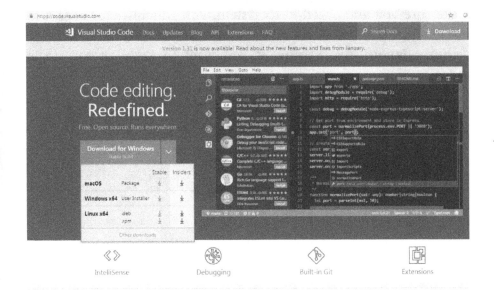

- Once you have downloaded Visual Studio code installer for your operating system, follow below steps to install the correct workload:

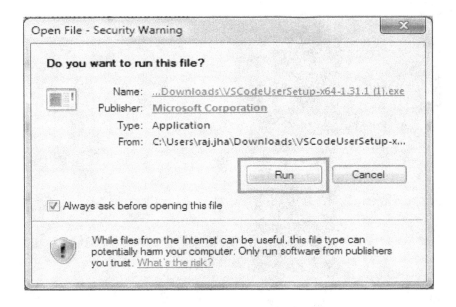

Make sure you are logged-in to system with administrator access to install visual studio code for all the users else you might get following warning. Ignore this warning if you want to install it for single user.

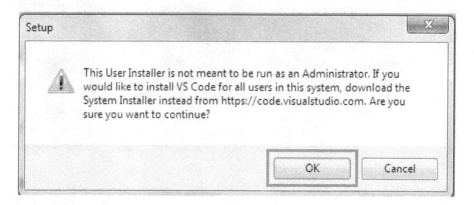

Proceed on other installation steps with default settings. Finish installation and launch visual studio code.

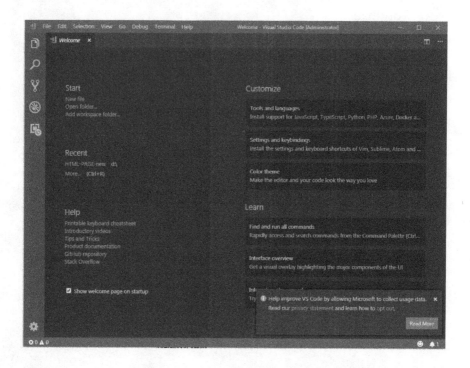

Click on extension icon at left panel and then search solidity extension for installation. Please be aware, we are using "JuanBlanco. solidity" extension. With this solidity extension, you can compile solidity code, highlight syntax along with having support for multiple solidity versions. To understand all the benefits you must read - https://marketplace.visualstudio.com/items?itemName=JuanBlanco. solidity

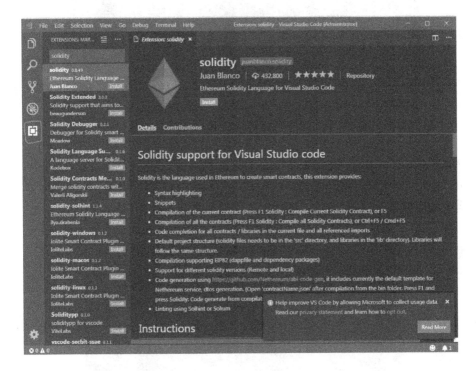

Search for 'material icon theme' on same extension search window and install this extension to render icons based on material design for visual studio ode.

After installation of material icon theme, we need to set the preferences in editor to use material icon theme. To accomplish this, go to File => Preferences => File Icon Theme => and select "material icon theme".

Now we are ready with visual code environment for solidity code development. Time to do practical for hands-on comprehension of solidity starting next chapter.

CHAPTER 2

Solidity Basics

In this chapter, we will traverse the journey that will make readers familiar with Solidity concepts with the help of crisp recipes. This is a practical book hence we recommend readers to try these recipes on their setup to make best use of this book. Get ready for a delightful extravagance as we will unfold several short recipes that encompass below concepts:

- Building layout of solidity File

- Define Boolean value type

- Define integer value type

- Define address value type

- Define dynamically sized value types

- Define fixed sized value type

- Define Enum value type

- Define different operators in solidity

- Define Array reference type

- Define Struct reference type

- Define Mapping reference type

- Define data structures in solidity

- Create Queue using solidity

- Create stack using solidity

- Define control structure in solidity

- Define Public and Internal Function Type

- Define External Function Type

- Define solidity functions modifiers

Technical Requirements

Setup Coding Environment

- Install visual studio code for Windows/Linux/Mac from https://code.visualstudio.com/

- Install Solidity visual studio code extension from visual studio market place - https://marketplace.visualstudio.com/items?itemName=JuanBlanco.solidity

- Install extension for material icon theme

First Recipe

Below code recipe is to write a short smart contract to approve or reject school trip plan. Let's start real action.

//Use latest pragma version to execute our code on https://remix.ethereum.org

```
pragma solidity ^0.5.1;

contract SchoolTrip{
bool public tripDecider;

//boolean variable that will initiate with default value false;
```

```solidity
function tripAnalyzer(uint256 studentCount, bool principleApproval, bool
legalApproval) internal pure returns(bool)
{
   /*Trip Decider Logic
   Operators && and || adhere to the common short-circuit rules
   i.e if expression is a(x) || b(y) then expression a(x) gets
   evaluated; which returns true and b(y) expression will not be
   evaluated
   */
   return (studentCount >= 100 && (principleApproval || legalApproval));
}

function checkTripStatus() public returns(bool)
   {
      // Add custom business logic here
      return tripDecider = tripAnalyzer(100,true,false);
   }
}
```

- Go to 'Run' tab on top right section

- Inside 'Run' choose environment in the dropdown to 'JavaScript VM'. There are three environments that can be interspersed with Remix as given below:

Javascript VM

Injected provider

Web3 provider

Web3 provider needs ethereum node while injected provider needs Mist or Metamask as external tool dependencies. That said - JavaScript VM is one option that is user friendly since each executable runs on your browser having no dependency elsewhere thereby providing total control in your hands.

- As a next step, click on deploy button to deploy contracts to EVM.

- Deploy process will deploy contract to blockchain and create contract instance where methods to run contract can be accessed.

- Thereafter execute function 'checkTripStatus' to see output in Remix console.

- You can smile if you witness output as 'True'.

- Congratulations, your school trip has been granted by smart contract. Do not forgot to include us in the expedition. ☺

- Please see screenshot of combined steps below.

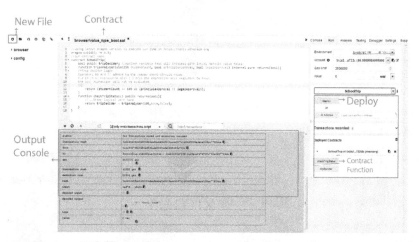

- You can follow above steps to deploy and run any solidity contract code you write.

Layout of Solidity File

Comprehension of code written by other developers can be tricky due to unfamiliar code styles and lack of standardization. We recommend standardization of basic code construct at the very least leading to consistency, comprehension and maintainability of code.

By reading this section, readers can understand solidity file layout standards from top-level declaration, contract level code structure and order of functions inside contract.

Typically order at meta-level is:

Pragma

Import

- Smart contract declaration

- State variables

- Events and modifiers

- Data structures

- Constructor

- Functions

- Default function [Optional]

Please refer to furnished sample layout file to standardize solidity code within your organization.

Pre Deep Dive Considerations

We recommend to create a folder in your computer drive and name it 'solidity_programming_concepts-samples'. Thereafter create separate folder for each chapter in order to save all sample contracts that you will write and experiment while reading this chapter.

Open a new file in VSCode. Create a new file and name it as 'solidityfilelayout_0.sol'. As we are creating this new file to comprehend solidityandfilelayoutstandardshencekeepfilenameas'solidityfilelayout_0. sol' where '.sol' is established extension of solidity file.

Code Recipes for Practical Learning

Nomenclature best practices advocate, 'Name of contract and library should match corresponding filenames'. In first few chapters we will not be too much fuzzy about this convention. We will keep file name based on topic or chapter name for better percolation of concepts thereby avoid dwelling too much into nomenclature verbatim.

We recommend using CapWords style convention for solidity contract name. Examples: MyFirstContract, FictitiousBank, Player, Champion, Owned so on and so forth".

Disclaimer – Style conventions are subject to change based on style guideline followed by organizations/entities for consistency however, any style guideline should abide compiler specific standards of language unconditionally.

We have segregated solidity file structure into two sections

1) Top-level declaration and 2) Layout inside contract.

1) Top-level declaration:

```
/*
    @INFO - Top level declaration in solidity file.
*/
pragma solidity ^0.4.23; //To indicate that this source code is not intended
to be compiled with a compiler earlier than version 0.4.23 and with 0.5.0
and higher (this second condition is added by using ^).
pragma solidity >=0.4.23 < 0.6.0; //To indicate that this source code will
work with compiler version 0.4.23 and above but not work if version 0.6.0
and above.
pragma solidity 0.4.23; //To lock the contract compiler for 0.4.23.

//Will import all symbols from "otherfile" into the current global scope.
import "otherfile.sol";
```

```
//Creates a new global symbol customSymbolName whose members are all
symbols from " otherfile.sol".
import * as symbolName from "otherfile.sol";
//Creates new global symbols alias and symbol2 which reference symbol1
and symbal2 from "otherfile.sol" respectively.
import {symbol1 as alias, symbol2} from "otherfile.sol"
//Same as import * as symbolName from "otherfile.sol";
import "otherfile.sol" as symbolName;

//Other import examples.
//Importing contract from other folder path.
import "other_folder/another_test.sol";
//Import from npm package folder
import "openzeppelin-solidity/contracts/ownership/Ownable.sol";

//Importing from relevant sources
import   "https://github.com/OpenZeppelin/openzeppelin-solidity/blob/
master/contracts/ownership/Ownable.sol";
import "git://github.com/<path>";
import "github.com/<path>";

//Example code to understand use of Import statement.
//npm install openzeppelin-solidity.
pragma solidity ^0.4.23;
import "openzeppelin-solidity/contracts/token/ERC20/ERC20.sol";
import   "openzeppelin-solidity/contracts/token/ERC20/ERC20Detailed.
sol";
contract ExampleToken is ERC20, ERC20Detailed {};

//This is single line comment.
/*This is multi
  line comment */
```

2) Layout inside contract:

```solidity
pragma solidity ^0.5.1;
//Ordering inside contract:
contract layoutSetter {

    /* State Variables
       Events
       Function Modifiers
       Value and Reference Types : Struct, arrays or Enum
       Constructor
       Fallback function (if exists)
       External
       Public
       Internal
       Private
       Default Fallback Functions
    */
    // State Variables
    address public stateVariable1;
    uint public stateVariable2;
    address owner;
    address mortal;

    // Events
    event Event1(address param1, uint param2);
    event Event2(address param1);
    event Event3();

    // Function Modifiers
    modifier onlyOwner {
        require(msg.sender == owner);
        _;
    }
```

```solidity
modifier onlyIfMortalModifier() {
    require(msg.sender == mortal);
    _;
}


// Value and Reference Types : Struct, arrays or Enum if any here
enum enum1 { val1, val2, val3 }
struct Person {
    uint name;
    uint addr;
    address location;
}
mapping (address => uint) balances;


// Define constructor here
constructor() public {
    // Initialize state variables here
}


// External functions
function externalFun() external pure returns(string memory){
    return "External function get called";
}


// External functions that are constant
function externalViewFun() external pure returns(string memory){
    return "External constant function get called";
}


// Public functions
function publicViewConstantFun() public pure returns(string memory){
    return "Public function get called";
}


// Internal functions
function internalFun() internal pure returns(string memory){
    return "Internal function get called";
```

```
}

// Private functions
function a() private pure returns(string memory){
   return "private function get called";
}

//Default or fallback function
function() external{
   revert();
   //Transaction should revert to initial state
}

}
```

Disclaimer – Following files have been furnished for demonstration purpose to comprehend structure of file. Please do not execute them directly on Remix. To understand and execute various sections, please go through this section meticulously.

Compiler Version: Pragmas

Let's write first layout file 'SolidityFileLayout.sol'.

The first line of contract is compiler version. Solidity provides warning at compilation stage if compiler version is not defined in solidity file.

```
SolidityFileLayout.sol
1    //contract with no pragrma or compiler version
2    contract A{}

PROBLEMS  2    OUTPUT    DEBUG CONSOLE    TERMINAL

  SolidityFileLayout.sol  D:\blockchain\Training\BTA Books\Code-Samples
     pragma-on-top: No Pragma directive found at the top of file. [2, 1]
```

At a broader level, three methods can be used to define pragma in solidity contract file as depicted below:

```
SolidityFileLayout.sol
1    //pragma solidity ^0.4.23;
2    //pragma solidity >=0.4.23 < 0.6.0;
3    //pragma solidity 0.4.23;
```

```
pragma solidity ^0.4.23;
```

Indicates that this source code is not intended to be compiled with a compiler version earlier than 0.4.23 and beyond 0.5.0 (^ is used to add second condition).

```
pragma solidity >=0.4.23 < 0.6.0;
```

Indicates that this source code will work with compiler version 0.4.23 and above but not work if version surpasses 0.6.0 or beyond.

```
pragma solidity 0.4.23;
```

Indicates compiler version to be used is 0.4.23 only. Mapping the pragma to version 0.4.23 ensures that contracts do not get compiled with more recent versions that may have different semantics leading to higher risks of undiscovered bugs. Likewise, older compiler versions are considered unsafe due to deprecated APIs.

Note: We need to add pragma directive in all the files in a project as it is always local to individual source file. Even importing another contract from base contract does not automatically apply pragma version of imported contract to new one. Please be cognizant of this.

Importing files

Although 'export' statement is not available in solidity however it does support 'import' statement. Below are the different methods that can be used to import a file in solidity:

Path Resolution

/	Directory Separator
.	Current directory
..	Parent Directory

Other import topologies are:

```
//Importing contract from other folder path
import "other_folder/another_test.sol";
//Import from npm package folder
import "openzeppelin-solidity/contracts/ownership/Ownable.sol";

//Importing from other sources
import "https://github.com/OpenZeppelin/openzeppelin-solidity/blob/
master/contracts/ownership/Ownable.sol";
import "git://github.com/<path>";
import "github.com/<path>";
```

In above section, we did ponder over several techniques to import files from different sources. Let's go through a practical use-case to understand use of importing files from other sources:

Suppose you have to implement a token in the organization namely 'MyCompanyToken'. Instead of writing token framrwork from scratch, you may want to reuse off-the-shelf token contract from a credible open-source framework such as 'OpenZeppelin' using npm install procedure. Try 'import' statement to import contracts from 'OpenZeppelin'. The code snippet we can use has been furnished below:

```
//npm install openzeppelin-solidity
pragma solidity ^0.4.23;
import "openzeppelin-solidity/contracts/token/ERC20/ERC20.sol";
import "openzeppelin-solidity/contracts/token/ERC20/ERC20Detailed.sol";
contract ExampleToken is ERC20, ERC20Detailed {}
```

Comments

In solidity, single-line comments are added using // while multi-line comments can be added using /*...*/.

```
//This is single line comment
/*This is multi
 line comment */
```

Maintaining order inside a contract:

In this section, we are providing guideline to organize elements inside contracts in right order based on our experience and recommended best practices.

That being said - Feel free to maintain style guide basis organization's recommendations.

Let's create a new file with VScode and name it 'SolidityFileLayout. sol'.

```
State Variables
Events
Function Modifiers
Struct, arrays or Enum
Constructor
Fallback function (if exists)
External
Public
Internal
Private
Default Functions
```

Example:

```
pragma solidity ^0.5.1;
//Logical ordering inside contract:
contract layoutSetter {
```

```
/* State Variables
   Events
   Function Modifiers
   Value and Reference Types : Struct, arrays or Enum
   Constructor
   Fallback function (if exists)
   External
   Public
   Internal
   Private
   Default Fallback Functions
*/
// State Variables
address public stateVariable1;
uint public stateVariable2;
address owner;
address mortal;

// Events
event Event1(address param1, uint param2);
event Event2(address param1);
event Event3();

// Function Modifiers
modifier onlyOwner {
   require(msg.sender == owner);
   _;
}

modifier onlyIfMortalModifier() {
   require(msg.sender == mortal);
   _;
}

// Value and Reference Types : Struct, arrays or Enum if any here
enum enum1 { val1, val2, val3 }
struct Person {
```

```solidity
    uint name;
    uint addr;
    address location;
}
mapping (address => uint) balances;

// Define constructor here
constructor() public {
  // Initialize state variables here
}

// External functions
function externalFun() external pure returns(string memory){
    return "External function get called";
}

// External functions that are constant
function externalViewFun() external pure returns(string memory){
    return "External constant function get called";
}

// Public functions
function publicViewConstantFun() public pure returns(string memory){
    return "Public function get called";
}

// Internal functions
function internalFun() internal pure returns(string memory){
    return "Internal function get called";
}

// Private functions
function a() private pure returns(string memory){
    return "private function get called";
}

//Default or fallback function
function() external{
```

```
    revert();
    //Transaction should revert to initial state
  }

}
```

Additional Context

To make our solidity code more readable, follow below solidity style guideline with VSCode or other editors:

- Recommend 4 spaces at each indentation level

- Top-level declarations in solidity source should be appended with two blank lines

- Within a contract, function declarations should be followed by a single blank line

- Maximum line length should be 79

- UTF-8 or ASCII encoding is preferred

See full guideline from official solidity source doc: https://solidity. readthedocs.io/en/v0.5.3/style-guide.html

Value Types in Solidity

Code recipes in this section will help readers comprehend how solidity deals with various value types with the help of easy to understand code snippets. In addition – Readers can use these practice tutorials to jump start in order to run sample solidity contracts on Remix online editor thereby saving precious time and effort.

Important Considerations

By design, every variable type in Solidity must be specified at compile time.

Value types are passed by value hence they are always explicitly copied.

Types can interact within this group in expressions comprising operators.

Undefined or null values do not exist in Solidity, default value however is dependent on the type.

Pre Deep Dive Considerations

Beginning from this section, every code snippet needs to be deployed on EVM for execution. Until now, we had setup VScode to write and compile code. To deploy our code on EVM, setup on local ethereum blockchain environment using Truffle (https://truffleframework. com/) and Ganache is recommended (https://truffleframework.com/ docs/ganache/quickstart).

As an alternative - Remix online IDE can be used that encapsulates underneath complexities from readers. We can test, debug and deploy solidity code online using Remix.

Refer "Technical Requirements" section to understand how we can compile and run solidity code on Remix online editor.

Recommendation: Since this is a practical grounds up book for passionate audience hence to reap maximum benefits, try every code snippet yourself to learn the rules of the game and play better than anybody else under the sun!

Background

Solidity being statically typed language appoints a type system that allows compiler to check correct usage of variables. Solidity compiler warrants every variable to be defined at compile time. Similar to statically typed languages such as C++, Java, C# so on and so forth, Solidity has both Value (Basic) type and Reference (Complex) type variables. If variable stores its own data then it is of value type. If it references location of data then it is a reference type.

Value Types: Value type variables are always passed by value. Variables get copied in memory when they are used as function arguments or via assignment. Let's ponder over various value types in solidity through code recipes.

Boolean value type: In solidity, Boolean types are supported with verbatim bool and possible values are true or false.

Example: A school needs to decide whether they can take their students for a trip. Many criteria need to be fulfilled to plan this trip seamlessly:

- Approval from either the principal or legal team

- Students count should not be less than 100

Let's open our file 'value_type_bool.sol' in VScode and write solidity code that approves or rejects school trip.

```solidity
//Using latest pragma version to execute our code on https://remix.
ethereum.org
pragma solidity ^0.5.1;
//Contract name
contract SchoolTrip{
  bool public tripDecider; //Boolean variable will initiate with initial default
value as false
  //Pure keyword - function will not alter the storage and even not read
storage state
    //Internal keyword – Only accessible to this contract and contracts
deriving from this contract
    function tripAnalyzer(uint256 studentCount, bool principleApproval,
bool legalApproval) internal pure returns(bool){
    /*Trip decider logic
    Operators && and || adhere to the common short-circuit rules.
    i.e if in an expression a(x) || b(y) the expression a(x) evaluates to true,
    the b(y) expression will not be evaluated
    */
    return (studentCount >= 100 && (principleApproval || legalApproval));
    }
  function checkTripStatus() public returns(bool){
    //Other logical snippet to be added here
```

```
      return tripDecider = tripAnalyzer(100,true,false);
   }
}
```

Few keywords in the contract may probably be new for you. Carefully read comments in solidity contract to keep a tab on all new terms for your own benefit. We will explain these keywords in later parts of the book as recap and ready reference.

Integer value type:

Solidity can administer integers (up to 256 bit, signed or unsigned) with fixed point numbers for development (in the form of ufixed/fixed type) without any solid plans for floating point implementation. An integer is declared with the keyword int or uint for unsigned integers.

- Normal integer declaration called 'int' ranges between -128 and 127

- Unsigned Integer 'uint' ranges between 0-255 however does not store any negative values

- Uint is alias for uint256 and int is alias of int256

Arithmetic operations with integer need careful scrutiny at a granular level as it can lead to integer overflow or underflow error and may terminate code abruptly. In following example, named as 'Safe-math', library can deal with overflow or underflow errors to ensure seamless code execution.

When maximum value ($2^{256}-1$) of unsigned integer increases by 1 then its value becomes zero and this triggers integer overflow.

```
uint256 maximumValue = 2**256-1; // maximumValue variable has
maximum value that an unsigned integer can hold
maximumValue += 1; // maximumValue has 0 value
```

If unsigned integer variable with value zero is decreased by 1 then its value breaches stipulation an integer can hold i.e. (2^{256}-1) leading to integer underflow.

```
uint256 minimumValue = 0; // minimumValue has 0 value
minimumValue -= 1; // It has 2**256-1 value
```

Let us analyze a simple smart contract that looks nice and simple but can cause havoc. Watch carefully, balances[msg.sender] – _value >= 0 condition is always satisfied because uint minus uint operation always renders a uint. uint is always greater or equal to 0. Hope the penny dropped in your brain!

Create a file 'value_type_integers_0.sol'.

```
pragma solidity ^0.5.1;
contract InsecureIntegerFlow{
    mapping (address => uint256) public balanceOf;

    // Vulnerable piece of code
    function transfer(address _to, uint256 _value) public { //Try with arguments
(0xca35b7d915458ef540ade6068dfe2f44e8fa733c,200) on remix.
        balanceOf[msg.sender] = 100; //Set balance of code executer address
to 100.
        /*
balances[msg.sender] – _value >= 0 condition is always satisfied because
uint minus uint operation always returns uint and uint is always greater or
equal to 0.

We have set sender address balance to 100. Check transfer occurs only when
sender has sufficient balance to send money i.e balanceOf[msg.sender] -
_value >= 0. Due to integer overflow that we explained above, condition
balanceOf[msg.sender] - _value >= 0 is always true thus sender can transfer
any amount to destination address.*/
        require(balanceOf[msg.sender] - _value >= 0); //This line of code can
create disaster or havoc.
        /* Add and subtract new balances */
        balanceOf[msg.sender] -= _value;
        balanceOf[_to] += _value;
    }
}
```

We will discuss many integer overflow and underflow scenarios with potential safeguards in depth while explaining security aspects of smart contract. For now - Look at correct way to write transfer function in contract as given below:

Create a file 'value_type_integers_1.sol'.

```solidity
pragma solidity ^0.5.1;
contract SecureIntegerFlow{
    mapping (address => uint256) public balanceOf;

    // Secure Version
    function transfer(address _to, uint256 _value) public {
    /* Check if sender has balance
      Thank God no overflow here.
    */
    require(balanceOf[msg.sender] >= _value && balanceOf[_to] + _value >=
balanceOf[_to]);
      /* Add and subtract new balances */
      balanceOf[msg.sender] -= _value;
      balanceOf[_to] += _value;
}
}
```

Address Value Type:

On the Ethereum blockchain, every account and smart contract has an address that is stored as 20-bytes. Address is used to send and receive ethers across accounts. This can be considered as public identity or account number on Blockchain for ready reference of transacting entities while masking underneath complexities making it secure.

Solidity has two address types, address and address payable. Both address and address payable stores 20-byte values. Difference however is address payable has additional functions i.e. transfer and send.

Address type is defined with 'address' keyword.

Example: Get contract executer associated with current contract

Create file 'value_type_address.sol'.

```solidity
pragma solidity ^0.5.1;
contract AddressGetter {
function getCallerAddresses() public view returns (address caller, address
contract1) {
//No arguments needed here
caller = msg.sender;
//Get caller address
contract1 = address(this);
//Retrieve contract address
return (caller,contract1);
}
}
```

Address payable has an additional keyword 'payable'. Use address payable to transfer funds from one account to another. There are two functions available to perform transfer i.e. send and transfer. Both are same and deal is when the transaction gets failed due to known or unknown reasons, 'send' returns a false flag whereas 'transfer' throws an exception and stops the execution immediately thereafter.

Create file 'value_type_address_1.sol'.

```solidity
pragma solidity ^0.5.1;
contract FundTransferer {
function Fundtransferer(address payable _address, uint amount) public {
//Try argument (0x14723a09acff6d2a60dcdf7aa4aff308fddc160c,100)
_address.transfer(amount);
//Use of transfer is preferred because it throws an exception and stops the
execution
}
function FundSender(address payable _address,
uint amount) public returns(bool){ //Try argument
(0x14723a09acff6d2a60dcdf7aa4aff308fddc160c,100)
_address.send(amount);
//Send returns false if error is detected
}
}
```

We can convert 'address payable' to 'address' implicitly but reverse is not possible although we can achieve this using an intermediate conversion to uint160.

Member methods associated with address are balance, call, callcode and delegatecall.

Balance – We can query balance of an address using this property and to send ether (in units of wei) to another address using transfer function.

Create file 'value_type_address_2.sol'.

```solidity
pragma solidity ^0.5.1;
contract FundTransferer {
    function Fundtransferer(address payable _address, uint amount) public {
//Try argument (0x14723a09acff6d2a60dcdf7aa4aff308fddc160c,100)
        address myAddress = address(this); //Contract address
        if (_address.balance < 10 && myAddress.balance >= 10) { //Check balance of sender and receiver(contract address) and then transfer to contract address.
        _address.transfer(amount);
    }
}
}
```

To comprehend difference between call, callcode and delegatecall, we need to understand different ways using which contracts can interact. Functions are there to interact with functions that do not have Application Binary Interface (ABI). These functions need special attention in programming because it can compromise safety and security of the contracts that makes them vulnerable for sabotage.

More to be served in the reader's platter while addressing 'Smart contract interaction techniques' later in the book to spice up this conversation so we are keeping additional context on the backburner for now. Let's go incremental to absorb concepts gradually.

Dynamically sized value types - String and Bytes

In solidity, bytes are used for arbitrary length raw byte data and string is for arbitrary length string (UTF-8) data.

Bytes: This is similar to byte[] however packed tightly in calldata.

String: String and bytes are alike however string does not allow index access.

Solidity best practices always recommend using bytes over string. There are many reasons behind it and prominent ones are listed below:

- Date should be of fixed sized during exchange between the contracts hence dynamically sized arrays such as strings, exchange is compromised. With bytes, we will be able to put them into a fixed size array; which allows percolation to other contracts

- Solidity (known until - version 0.4.19) is still unable to return string as function's result

- Bytes are less expensive due to lesser gas consumption compared to string

Most recommended way is to convert string to bytes32 when we need to pass any string value from one contract to another. Below is sample code that demonstrates conversion of string of less than 32 characters into bytes32.

Create file 'value_type_string_byte.sol'

```
pragma solidity ^0.5.1;
contract StringLessthen32CharecterToByte32 {
//Conversion of string less than 32 characters long to bytes32
   function toBytes32(string memory _string) public pure returns (bytes32)
{//Try argument ("Rendezvous with Practical Solidity")
      // Pure means we are neither accessing state nor changing it
      // Make sure string should be of less than 32 characters
```

```
      require(bytes(_string).length <= 32);
      bytes32 _stringBytes;
      //Best way of conversion from string to bytes32
      assembly {
        // Load the memory pointer of string with an offset of 32
        // 32 passes over non-core data parts of string such as length of text
        _stringBytes := mload(add(_string, 32))
        }
      return _stringBytes;
    }
}
```

Let's ponder over another sample to compare gas usage between string and bytes32.

Create file 'value_type_string_byte_1.sol'.

```
pragma solidity ^0.5.1;
contract GasUsesforBytesAndStrings {
    string constant _string = "Solidity Cook Book";
    /*
    For bytes32 constant _bytes keep string character less than 32 else you
    would get compilation error.
    */
    bytes32 constant _bytes = 'Solidity Cook Book';
    function getString() public pure returns(string memory) {
      return _string;
    }

    function getBytes() public pure returns(bytes32) {
      return _bytes;
    }
}
```

Verify for yourself in your environment, unambiguous inference shall be getString() consumes more gas than getBytes().

When code recipe was executed on Remix (https://remix. ethereum.org), following results were seen in Remix output console:.

Transaction cost for getBytes() was 21468 gas (Cost only applies when called by a contract)

Transaction cost for getString() was 21989 gas (Cost only applies when called by a contract)

Fixed sized value type - bytes1 (byte), bytes2, bytes3... bytes32:

Fixed size byte arrays are declared using keyword byte X where X is any number from 1 to 32. The keyword byte is alias for byte1. Fixed size arrays has '.length' for yielding the fixed size of the byte array. In the same note - please be aware of this being read-only.

Create file 'fixed_sized_bites.sol'.

```
pragma solidity ^0.5.1;
//Contract to return multiple sized bytes values.
contract BytesMultiReturner {
    function getData() public pure  returns (uint8, uint8) {
        bytes8 a = "Solidity"; //Size of 8.
        bytes32 b = "Rendezvous with Practical Solidity Book" //Size of 32.
        return (a.length, b.length); //Length will return uint value.
    }
}
```

Enum:

In solidity, Keyword 'enum' is used to declare enumerations; which represents user-defined data types. Enum consists of an enumeration list, a predetermined set of named constants. Enum supports explicit conversion to and from all integer types but does not allow implicit conversion. The explicit conversions check value ranges at runtime and failure renders an exception. At the very least, Enums must encompass one member.

Create file 'value_type_enum.sol'.

```
pragma solidity ^0.5.1;
//Create cars based on customer customization and default options.
contract CustomerCustomizationForCar {
//Enum assignment
enum WheelsChoices {
Alloy,Steel
} //Available wheels options
enum ColorChoices {
red,blue,orange,gray,white,yellow
}//Available color options
enum RoofChoices {
Hardtops,Sunroofs,Ttops,Targa,Vinyl
} //Available roof options

    WheelsChoices constant defaultWheel = WheelsChoices.Steel; //Default
car wheel
    ColorChoices constant defaultColor = ColorChoices.red; //Default car
color
    RoofChoices constant defaultRoof = RoofChoices.Hardtops; //Default
car roof

    //Create cars using struct. We will see Struct in subsequent sections
    struct CustomizedCar {
        string vin; //Car identification number
        WheelsChoices wheel; //Wheel chosen
        ColorChoices color; //Colour chosen
        RoofChoices roof; //Roof type chosen
    }

        mapping(string => CustomizedCar) customerCarMapping; //Keep
mapping of cars
    //Create car with customer selected options
    function createCustomizedCarForCustomer(string memory vin) public {
//Try any unique string as argument i.e ("111")
        customerCarMapping[vin] = CustomizedCar(vin,WheelsChoices.
Steel,ColorChoices.yellow,RoofChoices.Vinyl);
    }

    //Create car with default available options
    function createDefaultCarForCustomer(string memory vin) public { //
Try any unique string as argument i.e ("222")
```

```
    customerCarMapping[vin] =
    CustomizedCar(vin,defaultWheel,defaultColor,defaultRoof);
  }

  //Retrieve car information
  function getCar(string memory vin) public view returns
(uint256,uint256,uint256) { //Fetch using unique string i.e ("111") or
("222")
    //Enum is convertible to integer
    return (uint256(customerCarMapping[vin].
wheel), uint256(customerCarMapping[vin].
color),uint256(customerCarMapping[vin].roof));
  }
 }
}
```

Additional Context

There are few more value types in solidity as described below:

Hash

256-bit, 32-byte data chunk, indexable into bytes and operatable with
bitwise operations. This links one block to the adjacent block.

```
if(keccak256(streamm) == keccak256("Science"))
```

Fixed Point Numbers

fixed / ufixed: Fixed point number of various sizes for signed and
unsigned that can have decimal. Solidity has no solid plan for this till
date but surely intend is to support fixed point numbers in future.

Operators in Solidity

In Solidity, there are broadly five categories of operators namely:

    Comparison
    Arithmetic
    Logical
    Bitwise
    Shift

These five categories are unique and have diverse application in writing smart contracts. Code recipes in this section will practically demonstrate how developers can use solidity operators in code with relative ease and efficiency to develop pertinent business logic. Learn best practices through these recipes to optimize the usage of operators.

Pre Deep Dive Considerations

Open a new file in VS code and name it as 'operators.sol'. Save this file to 'solidity_programming_ practical_samples' folder. We will use VScode to write our code and will run this code on Remix online editor.

Code Recipes for Practical Learning

Operators that are used in solidity are very similar to JavaScript. Prominent operators available in solidity are as follows:

Operators	Description
!	Logical Negation
&& (and)	Logical Conjunction
||	Logical disjunction
==	Equality Operator
!=	Inequality Operator
<=, <, ==, !=, >=, >	Comparison Operators
&, |, ^	Bitwise Operators
~	Bitwise Negation
<< (left shift), >> (right shift)	Shift Operators
+, -, *, /, %,**	Arithmetic operators

Logical Conjunction (&&) and Logical disjunction (||) follow short circuit rule. According to this rule if f(x) evaluates to true in expression f(x) || g(y) then g(y) will not get evaluated.

Let us execute code snippet directly on Remix –

Disclaimer – Sample contract below is for practice purpose. Output will vary based on furnished input. Please provide inputs carefully because exception and error handling is not done for this code snippet.

Open https://remix.ethereum.org

Link will open with one default.sol file. Click on '+' button on online editor to create new solidity file and name it as 'value_type_bool.sol'. Paste following code in there and save it (ctrl+s).

```solidity
pragma solidity ^0.5.1;
contract OperatorsCollection{
    //Arithmetic OperatorsCollection
    uint result;
    function add(uint num, uint num1) public returns (uint) {
        result = num + num1;
        return result;
    }
    function substract(uint num, uint num1) public returns (uint) {
        result = num - num1;
        return result;
    }
    function multiply(uint num, uint num1) public returns (uint) {
        result = num * num1;
        return result;
    }
    function devide(uint num, uint num1) public returns (uint) {
        result = num/num1;
        return result;
    }
    function modulo(uint num, uint num1) public returns (uint) {
        result = num % num1;
        return result;
    }
    function exponentiation(uint num, uint num1) public returns (uint) {
        result = num ** num1;
        return result;
    }
    //Logical OperatorsCollection
    function logicalchecks(uint num, uint num1) public pure returns (bytes32)
    {
        if(num >= num1){
            return "num is greater and equal to num1";
```

```solidity
    }
    if(num <= num1) {
        return "num is less and equal to num1";
    }
    if(num > num1){
        return "num is greater than num1";
    }
    if(num == num1){
        return "num is equal to num1";
    }
    if(num != num1){
        return "num is not equal to num1";
    }
    if(num > num1){
        return "num is greater than num1";
    }
    if(num > 10 && num1 < 10){
        return "follow short-circuiting rule";
    }
    if(num > 10 || num1 < 10){
        return "follow short-circuiting rule.";
    }
}
//Logical operators

function and(bytes1 num, bytes1 num1) public pure returns (bytes1) {
    return num & num1;
}

function or(bytes1 num, bytes1 num1) public pure returns (bytes1) {
    return num | num1;
}

function xor(bytes1 num, bytes1 num1) public pure returns (bytes1) {
    return num ^ num1;
}
//Shift operators
function shiftright(uint num, uint num1) public pure returns (uint) {
```

```
   return num >> num1;
 }
 function shifleft(uint num, uint num1) public pure returns (uint) {
   return num << num1;
 }
}
```

Additional Context

Unsigned math operations are at times unsafe. The following scenarios needs to be watched for as they can cause cataclysm in production:

- Multiplication of two unsigned integers; reverts on overflow

- Integer division of two unsigned integers truncating the quotient; reverts on division by zero

- Subtraction of two unsigned integers; reverts on overflow

- Addition of two unsigned integers; reverts on overflow

- Division of two unsigned integers and return of remainder (unsigned integer modulo); reverts on division by zero

Although we can handle these scenarios in our code but we recommend using open-source libraries like OpenZeppelin- SafeMath to rescue readers from unwanted and counter-productive scenarios that can impact contracts adversely.

Solidity Reference Types

Types that do not necessarily fit into 256 bits require special treatment hence advent of 'Reference Types' in Solidity. Please be cognizant of the fact that complex types require careful consideration or else we lose performance making the language unpopular for enterprise applications. Let's understand this rider with the help of recipes and you will realize why 'Reference Types' are life saver and protagonist of optimization in the world of Solidity.

Pre Deep Dive Considerations

Open a new file in VS code and name it as 'reference_types.sol'. Save this file to 'solidity_programming_practical_samples' folder. Paste following code snippet in file.

```solidity
pragma solidity ^0.5.1;
contract EmrPatients{
    // This is the Constructor and it gets called ONCE only when contract is
first deployed
    constructor() public {
    //Do nothing for now
    }
    //Define mapping to store key-value pairs
    mapping(string => medicalRecord) patientRecordMapping;


    //Organize medical records using struct
    struct medicalRecord
    {
        string report_name;
        address owner;
    }
    //Save medical record
    function saveMedicalReport(string memory mr_number, string memory
report_name, address p_addr) public payable {
        patientRecordMapping[mr_number] = medicalRecord(report_name,
p_addr);
    }

        function getReportByMedicalRecordNumber(string memory mr_
number) public view returns (string memory, address) {
            return (patientRecordMapping[mr_number].report_name,
patientRecordMapping[mr_number].owner);
    }
}
```

Array: Array is group of elements of the same type in which each individual element has a particular location called index. The size of arrays can be fixed or dynamic as needed.

```
uint[5] Reports; //Fixed sized array
uint[] Reports; //Dynamic sized array
```

Structs: In solidity, users can define their own types in form of structure. Struct keyword is used to define struct. Struct can encompass both value and reference types.

```
struct medicalRecord
  {
    string report_name;
    string report_url;
    address owner;
  }
```

Mapping: Mapping stores data in a key-value pair where key can be any built-in value type or [byte and string]

```
mapping(address => string[]) addressAccessOnReports;
```

Code recipe below appositely show-cases the collective power of reference types i.e. Array, Struct and Mapping. FYI...This smart contract allows creation and retrieval of electronic medical records for patients.

```
pragma solidity ^0.5.1;
contract EmrPatients{
    // This is the Constructor and it gets called ONCE only when contract is
first deployed
    constructor() public {
    //Do nothing for now
    }
    //Define mapping to store key-value pairs
    mapping(string => medicalRecord) patientRecordMapping;


    //Organize medical records using struct
```

```
struct medicalRecord
{
   string report_name;
   address owner;
}
//Save medical record
function saveMedicalReport(string memory mr_number, string memory
report_name, address p_addr) public payable {
     patientRecordMapping[mr_number] = medicalRecord(report_name,
p_addr);
}

     function getReportByMedicalRecordNumber(string memory mr_
number) public view returns (string memory, address) {
          return (patientRecordMapping[mr_number].report_name,
patientRecordMapping[mr_number].owner);
}
}
```

Additional Context

Reference type or complex type needs to be handled very carefully due to following reasons:

- They do not necessarily fit into 256 bits

- Amount of gas used to execute a transaction depends on data location. Copying reference types are very expensive hence it is recommended that we should choose storage type between memory and storage for reference types.

- With a reference type, two different variables can reference the same location. As a result, any change in one variable will impact other one too.

- There are three types of storage available for reference type: memory, storage and calldata.

To learn more about different data storage available in solidity, keep a close tab on upcoming chapters. Happy learning!

Data Structures in Solidity

Solidity has simple approach when it comes to data structures. There are two basic data structures available that are apt for majority of the rudimentary or routine operations. Solidity has also provided an option to create custom data structure as deemed fit based on business need. In this section, we will ponder on basic data structures and additionally will go through few out-of-the-box custom data structures to give readers a food for thought. Let's get into action straightaway.

Pre Deep Dive Considerations

Open a new file in VS code and name it as 'datastrcture_1.sol'. Save this file to 'solidity_programming_practical_samples' folder.

Code Recipes for Practical Learning

Ideally, solidity provides only two data structures namely mapping and array. It is also possible to implement a new data structure over and above these two. The data structure can also be an amalgamation of mapping and array types where data can be stored in mapping with index assigned to it while tracking index through array data structure.

Practice time to see this working in real action. Code recipe below aims to accept donations from different addresses, do basic summation and retrieve total donation amount for audit trail. Address array 'allDoners' keeps keys for mapping and helps in the mapping traversal.

```
pragma solidity ^0.5.1;
contract DonationManager{
    // This is the Constructor and it gets called ONCE only when contract is
first deployed
    constructor() public {
    //Do nothing for now
    }
```

```
    //Define mapping to store key-value pairs. We cannot traverse mapping
so use conjunction with array
    mapping(address => uint) donarAmountMapping;
    //Array to store index of mapping data structure
    address[] allDoners;


    //Save donations from different addresses. Ensure no duplicity please!
    function getDonations(address donar, uint amount) public payable {
        donarAmountMapping[donar] = amount;
        allDoners.push(donar);
    }

    function iterateMapping() public view returns (uint) {
        uint totalDonation = 0;
    //Reset previous value as every time we need total count by traversing all
    donors
        for (uint i=0; i < allDoners.length; i++) {
            totalDonation += donarAmountMapping[allDoners[i]];
        }
        return totalDonation;
    }
}
```

Unlike other established programming languages, solidity does not provide complex data structures such as linked-list, queue so on and so forth. We can however create custom libraries and implement complex data structures leveraging existing available capability of solidity language. Let's build complex data structures to check the veracity of above stated facts.

Open a new file in VS code and name it as 'datastrcture_queue.sol'. Save this file to 'solidity_programming_practical_samples' folder.

```
pragma solidity ^0.5.1;
/*Although this is not an ideal way to implement queue however not too bad
at rudimentary level

//First in first out - Implemented this using mapping
```

```
contract QueueFIFO {
  mapping(uint256 => uint) queue;
//Mapping based queue
  uint256 first = 1;
  uint256 last = 0;
  //enqueue uint
  function enqueue(uint data) public {
    last += 1;
    queue[last] = data;
  }
  //dequeue uint
  function dequeue() public returns (uint data) {
    require(last >= first);
// Ascertain non-empty queue

    data = queue[first];

    delete queue[first];
    first += 1;
  }
}
```

Likewise, we can write code for stack, double-ended queue and linked-list. Custom algorithms to implement sorting, trees etc can also be accomplished emulating them. Let's ponder over another example where we will implement last-in-first-out stack using dynamic array.

Open a new file in VS code and name it as 'datastrcture_stack.sol'. Save this file to 'solidity_programming_practical_samples' folder.

```
pragma solidity ^0.5.1;

//Last-in first-out implementation.
contract StackLIFO {
  uint[] stack;
//Dynamic sized stack

  //Put uint elements in array
  function push(uint data) public {
    stack.push(data);
  }
```

```
function pop() public returns (uint data) {
    require(stack.length > 0);
//If stack is empty then do not try pop
    data = stack[stack.length - 1];
        //Delete pop element. Ideally this line is not required as last line will
delete element as well with decreasing array size. LOL
    delete stack[stack.length - 1];
    stack.length -= 1;
//Decrease array length by 1
    }
    //Retrive stack every time to see push pop after results
    function getStack() public view returns (uint[] memory){
        return stack;
    }
}
```

Additional Context

You can experiment more with code by implementing complex data structures using solidity code. We however recommend to use widely accepted and tested open-source libraries while using complex data structures in real projects so that nothing is left to chance. Smart contacts have to be smart. Hope you concur.

Another example: To use linked-lists use npm package 'solidity-linked-list' https://www.npmjs.com/package/solidity-linked-list

Solidity Control Structures

If you are familiar with JavaScript world, you can smile loud as you do not have to re-invent the wheel significantly. Most of the JavaScript control structures are available in Solidity with very few additions and omissions. Let's cruise through the concepts nevertheless without getting hands too much dirty with the help of crisp and concise recipes furnished in the coming section.

Pre Deep Dive Considerations

Open a new file in VS code and name it as 'control_structure.sol'. Save this file inside 'solidity_programming_practical_samples' folder.

Code Recipes for Practical Learning

Solidity provides all JavaScript like control statements except goto and switch. Control statements in its bandwagon are:

if, else, while, do, for, break, continue, return, ? :

while, do, for statements: These were devised to execute statements in loop; a loop is a set of controlled statements executed as part of a given condition or set of conditions.

break, continue: Break stops execution of loop and continue statement causes program to goto next leg of loop.

Return: This control structure is used to retrun the results to triggering code.

You can use the following code snippet directly on Remix online editor to understand control structures practically.

```solidity
pragma solidity ^0.5.1;
contract Math {

    function isDivisibleBy(uint dividend, uint divisor ) public pure  returns( bool ){
        // If statement will be executed provided given condition is true(bool)
        if((dividend % divisor) == 0){
            return true;
        }
        else {
            // This will be executed provided IF statement is false
            return false;
        }
        /*We can write above statement using conditional operator (? :) as well
          return bool flag = (dividend % divisor) == 0) ? true : false
        */

    }

    function getFactorial(uint number) public pure returns( uint ){
```

```
if(number == 0){ //If loop
    return 1; //Return result
}
else {
    uint factorial = 1;
    for(uint i = number;i>1;i--) //For loop
    {
        factorial = factorial * i;
        if(factorial > 100){
            break; //Terminate loop
        }
    }
    return factorial; //Return result
}
}
}
```

Additional Context

Instead of using if statement in "isDivisibleBy" method, we can use conditional operator as furnished below:

```
pragma solidity ^0.5.1;
contract Math {

    function isDivisibleBy(uint dividend, uint divisor ) public pure  returns( bool ){
        //We can write above statement using conditional operator (? :) as well
        return (dividend % divisor) == 0) ? true : false

    }
}
```

Assert, Require, Revert and Exceptions control execution of the program – Be wary of it. We have already demonstrated Require at number of places in our sample codes. See 'datastructure_stack.sol' where it was used very recently to refresh your memory. We will understand Assert, Require, Revert and Exceptions in depth in the subsequent chapters. Stay tuned!

Leaving you with yourself and one more example where 'require' can be practiced. In this example, you will also see how we can create object of one contract inside other.

Create file using VSCode "require.sol"

```solidity
pragma solidity ^0.5.1;
contract Math {
    //Check divisibility
    function isDivisibleBy(uint dividend, uint divisor ) external pure returns( bool, uint ){
        if((dividend % divisor) == 0){
            return (true, divisor);
        }
        else {
            return (false,divisor);
        }
    }
}
contract MathUser {
    Math util = new Math(); //Instance of Math contract
    function outputOfisDivisibleBy(uint balance) public view returns(bool,uint){
        require(balance > 2, "No balance to execute"); //If executor has less balance then render VM error
        util.isDivisibleBy(45,5);
    }
}
```

Try to deploy 'MathUser' contract using Remix. You will get shot down by following error in Remix console if 'outputOfisDivisibleBy' method parameter value is less than 2.

Solidity Functions

Function types have four topologies namely internal, external, public and private.

Internal : Can only be called inside the contract

External : Can be called from other contracts however not from within

Public : Can be called from anywhere

Private : Can only be called from within the contract

Let's ponder over these one by one using practical recipes.

Pre Deep Dive Considerations

Open a new file in VS code and name it as 'function_types_public_internal.sol'. Save this file to 'solidity_programming_practical_samples' folder.

In solidity, Functions can be depicted as follows

function (<parameter types>) {internal|external|public|private} [pure|view|
payable] [(modifiers)] [returns (<return types>)]

Best practice is to always explicitly postulate the visibility of functions. There are four function types in Solidity kitty to specify function visibility.

Anyone can call the function, It is part of contract Interface and can be either called internally or via messages. An automatic getter function is generated For public state variables.

Private functions and state variables are only visible for the contract they are defined in and not in derived contracts.

External functions are part of the contract interface, which means they can be called from other contracts and via transactions (DAPP). An external function f cannot be called internally (i.e. fOdoes not work, but this.f() works).

Those functions and state variables can only be accessed internally (i.e. from within the current contract or contracts deriving from it), without using this.

Code Recipes for Practical Learning

Let us understand function types using solidity code recipes furnished below:

Example:

Public and Internal Function Type: Create a file 'function_types_public_internal.sol' and try following code.

```
pragma solidity ^0.5.1;
contract Math {
    /* Anyone can call the function. Being part of contract interface, it can be
called internally or via messages. An automatic getter function is generated
for public state variables.*/
    function getFactorial(uint number) public pure returns( uint ){
```

```
      return factorial(number); //Call internal function
   }


   //Can only be accessed internally (From within the current contract or
contracts deriving from it), without using this.
   function factorial(uint number) internal pure returns( uint ){
      if(number == 0) {
         return 1;
      } else {
         return number * factorial(number - 1);
      }
   }
}
```

External Function Type: Create a file "function_types_external.sol" and try following code.

```
pragma solidity ^0.5.1;
contract Math {

   function isDivisibleBy(uint dividend, uint divisor ) external pure returns(
bool ){
      if((dividend % divisor) == 0){
         return true;
      }
      else {
         return false;
      }
   }
}
contract MathUser {
   uint balance = 5;
   Math util = new Math();
   function outputOfisDivisibleBy() public view returns(bool){
      return util.isDivisibleBy(45,5);
   }
}
```

Additional Context

Solidity functions expect 'returns' keyword with all return types defined in functions at compile stage. Default storage for function and return argument is 'Memory'.

```
function isDivisibleBy(uint dividend, uint divisor ) external pure  returns( bool ){
```

Treat with different data types in depth awaits you in the upcoming chapters. Hold your thoughts for now!

Solidity Functions Modifiers

Function modifiers can alter function behavior with their unique application. These are inheritable and hence can be overridden by contracts extended from them. Interesting and intuitive application - Multiple modifiers can be applied to a function by separating them with whitespaces. Each modifier is evaluated in the furnished order. This feature is very useful is changing existing functions at mass scale in a less verbose and agile way. Let's understand this in depth with the help of crisp recipes.

Pre Deep Dive Considerations

Open a new file in VS code and name it as 'functions_modifiers.sol'. Save this file to 'solidity_programming_practical_samples' folder.

Code Recipes for Practical Learning

Modifiers can check result even before function execution and can change function's behavior. In addition, derived contract can override modifiers of parent contract.

VIEW

This modifier is used to view state of blockchain without altering it or its data. For your reference - It was referred as 'constant' in previous versions. It simply means function is 'Read-only'. Refer 'datastrcture_1.

sol' example to recap 'iterateMapping' function. Its purpose was to read data thus modifier 'view' was used.

```
function iterateMapping() public view returns (uint) {
    uint totalDonation = 0; //Reset old value as every time we need total
count by traversing all donors
    for (uint i=0; i < allDoners.length; i++) {
        totalDonation += donarAmountMapping[allDoners[i]];
    }
    return totalDonation;
}
```

PAYABLE

This modifier is used to indicate definite amount of ether/gas the transaction will incur. Refer 'datastrcture_1.sol' example. 'getDonations' function here is saving data on blockchain and changing the states.

```
//Save donations from different addresses. Ensure no duplicity hence please
check
    function getDonations(address donar, uint amount) public payable {
        donarAmountMapping[donar] = amount;
        allDoners.push(donar);
    }
```

PURE

This modifier neither reads nor writes to blockchain. It is used when given input always returns the same output come what may. Pure function returns a value using only the parameter of function without any impact on outer variable.

Refer 'datastrcture_1.sol' example for quick recap – If we write another function which only donation manager can use to get result based on mathematical calculation on input arguments then 'pure' has apt application here.

Create new file "datastructure_1_ext.sol".

```solidity
//This function will do calculation on arguments/parameters
    function calculateAmountAfterExpenses(uint amount, uint expense1,
uint expense2) public pure returns(uint){
        return amount = amount - (expense1 + expense2);
    }
```

Practice below code using remix online editor and play with different modifiers keeping a close tab on output especially compilation errors. There is a special saying 'We get wiser by experiences' - This holds true here.

Create new file "datastructure_1_ext.sol".

```solidity
pragma solidity ^0.5.1;
contract DonationManager{
    // This is the Constructor and it gets called ONCE only when contract is
first deployed
    constructor() public {
    //Do nothing for now
    }
    //Define  mapping to store key-value pairs. We cannot traverse mapping
thus use array
    mapping(address => uint) donarAmountMapping;
    //Array to store index of mapping data structure
    address[] allDoners;

    //Save donations from different addresses. Ensure no duplicity – Please
check
    function getDonations(address donar, uint amount) public payable {
        donarAmountMapping[donar] = amount;
        allDoners.push(donar);
    }

    function iterateMapping() public view returns (uint) {
        uint totalDonation = 0;
//Reset old value as every time we need total count by traversing all donors
        for (uint i=0; i < allDoners.length; i++) {
```

```
        totalDonation += donarAmountMapping[allDoners[i]];
    }
    return totalDonation;
}


    //This function will perform calculation on the provided arguments/
parameters
    function calculateAmountAfterExpenses(uint amount, uint expense1,
uint expense2) public pure returns(uint){
        return amount = amount - (expense1 + expense2);
    }
}
```

Additional Context

In solidity, we can also define custom modifiers. A custom modifier can be envisioned and emulated similar to a function.

```
modifier onlyOwner () {
    require(msg.sender == owner);
    _;
}

modifier isValueBiggerThanZero(uint value) {
    require(value > 0);
    _;
}
```

Summary

Hope you are now familiar with the turf on which you will be playing. Absorb these concepts and go through all examples yourself on Remix to connect all the dots. The more you sweat in training, the less you bleed in war. Once you are ready to chew more, we will move to real court from this virtual training chamber.

Fair Warning – Unlearn traditional programming language concepts and relearn as needed to avoid conjecture. Go learn the rules of game and play better than everybody else.

CHAPTER 3

A Tryst with Advanced Solidity Concepts

Introduction

In this chapter, we aim to accomplish below goals through diverse recipes:

- Comprehend contracts and their pertinent structure

- Show-case optimum techniques to interact with other contracts

Right structure helps achieve standardization and in turn leads to institutionalization of best practices across organization. This has several long-term benefits as organization contracts grow leaps and bounds.

There are potential caveats involved when one contract calls external contracts due to security vulnerabilities. Essentially, our focus for now will be on sharing right methodology and best practices rather than emphasizing too much on the caveats at this stage.

We will go through the following recipes:

- Solidity Function Calls

- Solidity Contracts and Inheritance

- Abstract and interface contracts

- Events in Solidity

- Library in Solidity

- Global variables in Solidity

- Solidity Assembly

- Using For Declarations

- Payable and Withdrawal

- Solidity Bytecode and Opcode

Technical Requirements

Basics of Blockchain and Canonical Understanding of Ethereum

Readers should know and understand the basics of blockchain -https://solidity.readthedocs.io/en/latest/introduction-to-smart-contracts.html#blockchain-basics

Readers should know about ethereum and ethereum virtual machine (EVM) -https://solidity.readthedocs.io/en/latest/introduction-to-smart- contracts.html#index-6

Setup Coding Environment

- Install visual studio code for Windows/Linux/Mac from https://code.visualstudio.com/

- Install Solidity visual studio code extension from visual studio market place -https://marketplace.visualstudio.com/items?itemName=JuanBlanco.solidity

- Install extension for material icon theme.

Solidity Function Calls

Solidity provides internal and external function calls. Internal function calls are within the same contract scope. To call a function from any other contract, we use an external function call. Let's go through both function types with the help of recipes and get full clarity on the usage and modalities involved in the process.

Pre Deep Dive Considerations

Launch the VS code editor to write and edit code blocks. We begin by creating a folder named solidity_programming_practical_samples. In the browser, open the Remix online editor to compile and run the recipe code blocks. In-depth details are explained in the next section.

Code Recipes for Practical Learning

1. Create following files in VScode:

    The Internal Function call "function_internal_call.sol" - To create recipe to understand solidity internal calls within contract, paste following code snippet into this file.

```solidity
pragma solidity ^0.5.1; contract Math {
/* Anyone can call this function. This is part of contract interface and can
be either called internally or via messages
An automatic getter function is generated for public state variables.*/
function getFactorial(uint number) public pure returns( uint ){
return factorial(number); //Call of internal function }
//Can only be accessed internally i.e. from within the current contract or
contracts deriving from it
function factorial(uint number) internal pure returns( uint ){ if(number
== 0) {
return 1; } else {
return number * factorial(number - 1); }
}
}
```

2. External Function call "function_external_call.sol" – This show-cases external calls to another contract using crisp and concise recipe. Please paste following code to file -

```solidity
pragma solidity ^0.5.1;
// No exception handling has done here. Recipe is just for quick demonstration purpose only
//Random logic to calculate insurance premium based on age, time duration, alcohol consumption status and smoking habit affirmation
contract InsurerCompany {
  //This method has defined payable only because we can show how we can pass gas while calling it
    function insuranceAmountCalculator(int age,bool is_smoke, bool is_consume_alcohol,int time_period) external payable returns (int insurance_amount) {
        int variable_amount = 0;
        if(is_consume_alcohol){
          variable_amount = variable_amount + 100;
        }
        if(is_smoke){
          variable_amount = variable_amount + 100;
        }
        return ((variable_amount + (age + 50)) - time_period); //Random logic to calculate insurance premium based on age, time duration, alcohol consumption status and smoking habit affirmation
    }

}


//Contract for insurance agent. Insurance agent to save client user info and calculate insurance premium using Insurer company contract
contract InsuranceAgent {
  InsurerCompany ic;
  constructor(address _ic) public {
```

```
        ic = InsurerCompany(_ic); //Assuming we know address of
InsurerCompany contract. Initialize third party contract in constructor
    }
    //Define mapping to store key-value pairs
    mapping(string => userRecord) userRecordMapping;

    //Organize user records using struct
    struct userRecord
    {
        string unique_identification;
        string name;
        int age;
        bool is_smoke;
        bool is_consume_alcohol;
        int time_period;
    }
    //Save user record. Test data to test on Remix -
("U123",20,"Jon",true,true,10)
    function saveUserDetails(string memory unique_identification, int age,
string memory name, bool is_smoke, bool is_consume_alcohol, int time_
period) public payable {
        userRecordMapping[unique_identification] = userRecord(unique_
identification, name, age, is_smoke, is_consume_alcohol, time_period);
    }

    //Retrieve insurance premium information using third party contract.
Test data to test on Remix - ("U123")
    function getInsurancePremium(string memory unique_identification)
public payable returns (int){
        /*
        value(msg.value) - send gas in wei unit to destination contract i.e
InsurerCompany.
        gas(1000) - Set gas limit modifier
        */
        return ic.insuranceAmountCalculator.value(msg.value).
gas(1000)(userRecordMapping[unique_identification].
age, userRecordMapping[unique_identification].is_smoke,
```

```
userRecordMapping[unique_identification].is_consume_alcohol,
userRecordMapping[unique_identification].time_period);
   }
}
```

Disclaimer – Read next section and code snippet comments inline to successfully execute it on Remix.

3. Run Remix Online Editor: Executing contract code from "function_internal_call.sol" is quite simple as it encompasses only one contract. That said – Executing contract code from "function_external_call.sol" is tricky. To execute it rather easily on remix, please follow below steps.

Note: Reading comments inside code snippets is equally important thus please do not overlook them.

4. Open https://remix.ethereum.org. Create a new.sol file and subsequently copy recipe code from your VScode file "function_internal_call.sol" and paste it into remix.sol file.

5. Go to 'Run' tab in the top right section.

6. Inside 'Run' choose environment in the dropdown to 'JavaScript VM'.

7. You will see two contract names in the dropdown inside deploy section. The two contracts are "InsurerCompany" and "InsuranceAgent". See screenshot below for more clarity:

8. The deployment order of contracts is extremely vital. Reason for this submission is the recipe code constructor where deploy address of "InsurerCompany" is being used while deploying "InsuranceAgent". Due to this repercussion, "InsurerCompany" should be deployed first. Choose "InsurerCompany" option from dropdown and deploy it. After deployment, copy the address of deployed contract. Refer to the screenshot below:

9. Now choose "InsuranceAgent" contract from dropdown and deploy it with address that you copied in the last step. Thereafter execute methods available in contract i.e "saveUserDetails" and "getInsurancePremium" with your own argument values. As an alternative, test argument data provided in the comment section of code. Refer screenshot below:

Code snippet in "function_internal_call.sol" file is our custom mathematical contract to calculate factorial of a given input number that we discussed earlier. In this contract we called factorial () function internally to another function named getFactorial() within the same contract. Hope this clarifies.

```
function getFactorial(uint number) public pure returns( uint ){ return
factorial(number); //Internal function call
}
```

Internal function calls do not require message call. This is rather a simple EVM jump from caller function to corresponding called function and hence no cost is associated with it.

"function_internal_call.sol" also demonstrates recursive function call within the same contract. See code snippet below:

```
function factorial(uint number) internal pure returns( uint ){ if(number
== 0) {
return 1; }
else {
return number * factorial(number - 1); }
}
```

Code recipe in "function_external_call.sol" contract consists of two contracts. Recipe demonstrates the interaction between two contracts deployed on the following two ethereum addresses on EVM:

- Contract InsurerCompany {}: InsuranceAgent contract is responsible to create users and fetch insurance premium amount for users based on parameters furnished by them. Parameters include age, smoking or alcohol consumption status and duration of insurance.

- Contract InsuranceAgent {}: InsuranceAgent contract relies on InsurerCompany to calculate premium for the user based on the given information. As a result, InsuranceAgent contract initializes an instance of contract InsurerCompany while deploying (inside Constructor()) to ethereum blockchain. Refer code snippet below to see this in action.

Please be cognizant of that fact that we can only initialize already deployed contract inside a new contract when we know the address of the previously deployed contract. Knowing ABI (Application Binary Interface) is also a mandatory step to be familiar with method and arguments deployed contract (InsurerCompany) expects from caller contract (InsuranceAgent).

```
contract InsuranceAgent { InsurerCompany ic; constructor(address _ic) public {
ic = InsurerCompany(_ic);
//Assuming we already know address of Insurer Company contract. Initialize third party contract in constructor seamlessly }
```

With the instance of contract InsurerCompany, InsuranceAgent calls the function insuranceAmountCalculator() from InsurerCompany with arguments and calculcates insurance premium amount.

Refer code snippet below to understand how this works:

```
//Fetch insurance premium information using third party contract. Test data to test on Remix is : ("U123")
function getInsurancePremium(string memory unique_identification) public payable returns (int){
/*
value(msg.value) - Send gas in wei unit to destination contract i.e Insurer Company.
gas(1000) - Set gas limit modifier. */
return                    ic.insuranceAmountCalculator.value(msg.value).
gas(1000)(userRecordMapping[unique_                identification].
age,                userRecordMapping[unique_identification].is_smoke,
userRecordMapping[unique_identification].is_consume_alcohol,
userRecordMapping[unique_identification].time_period);
}
```

From the preceding code, we observe the following:

- From code snippet, you will find "value(msg.value).gas(1000). Value(msg.value)" is used to send gas in Wei unit to destination contract i.e InsurerCompany. Gas(1000) modifier is used to set gas limit.

- These are required because we have defined "insuranceAmountCalculator()" function in InsurerCompany contract as "payable". This expects gas in wei unit to execute seamlessly.

- Please refer following code snippet : function insuranceAmountCalculator(int age,bool is_smoke, bool is_consume_alcohol,int time_period) external payable returns (int insurance_amount) { }

In the above code snippet, we have defined "insuranceAmountCalculator" with keyword "external" to make it callable from other contracts.

Additional Context

Function calls in solidity also support "named calls" for parameters. This is very useful when we do not have to maintain order of arguments. In solidity, we achieve this by passing named argument inside parenthesis{}. To provide a demonstration of named parameter calls within the function "insuranceAmountCalculator", we have hard coded named parameter values inside the function.

```
pragma solidity ^0.5.1;
/* No exception handling has been done here. This snippet is just for
demonstration purpose. Insurer company contract calculates premium
amount based on age, time period, alcohol and smoke consumption status.*/
contract InsurerCompany {
int constant base_amount = 100;
```

```
function insuranceAmountCalculator(int age,bool is_smoke, bool is_
consume_alcohol,int time_period) external payable returns (int insurance_
amount) {
int variable_amount = 0; if(is_consume_alcohol){
variable_amount = variable_amount + 100; }
if(is_smoke){
variable_amount = variable_amount + 100; }
return ((base_amount + variable_amount + (age + 50)) - time_period);
//Random logic to calculate insurance premium based on age, time duration,
alcohol consumption status and smoking habit affirmation
} }
/*
Contract for insurance agent is below; which calculates insurance premium
*/
contract InsuranceAgent {
InsurerCompany ic; constructor(address_ic) public { ic = InsurerCompany(_
ic);
/*Assuming we know address of InsurerCompany contract. Constructor
initializes third party contract*/
}
//Fetch insurance premium using third party contract function
getInsurancePremium() public returns (int){
return ic.insuranceAmountCalculator.gas(1000)({is_smoke: true, age: 30,
time_period: 30, is_consume_alcohol: false});//Named parameter calls
} }
```

Solidity Contracts and Inheritance

Contracts and Inheritance

Solidity supports inheritance in contracts by copying parent (base) contract bytecode into child (derived) contract bytecode. Finally a single unified contract is generated after deployment on EVM and single address is manifested in the process. Solidity supports several types of inheritance namely Single, Multi-level, Hierarchical and Multiple. Let's get our hands dirty and learn the concepts with the recipes that are show-cased in the upcoming section.

Pre Deep Dive Considerations

First of all, launch the VS code editor to write and edit code snippets. We begin by creating a folder named 'solidity_programming_practical_ samples'. In the browser, open the Remix online editor to compile and run the recipe code. In-depth details are explained in the next section.

Code Recipes for Practical Learning

1. Create following files in VScode:

    Single Inheritance "single_inheritance.sol" - To create recipe to demonstrate single inheritance.

```solidity
pragma solidity ^0.5.1;
contract HealthInsuranceAgent {
  constructor() public {
    //Do nothing for now
  }
  //Health insurance calculator
  int constant base_amount = 100;
    function insuranceAmountCalculator(int age,bool is_smoke, bool is_
consume_alcohol,int time_period) internal pure returns (int insurance_
amount) {
      int variable_amount = 0;
      if(is_consume_alcohol){
        variable_amount = variable_amount + 100;
      }
      if(is_smoke){
        variable_amount = variable_amount + 100;
      }
      return ((base_amount + variable_amount + (age + 50)) - time_period);
//Random logic to calculate insurance amount based on age, time period,
alcohol consumption state and smoking habit affirmation
    }
```

```
    function checkEligibility(int age, int time_period) internal pure returns
(bool is_insurance_possible) {
        //Random logic for insurance eligibility. You can make your own
version :)
        if (age > 60 || time_period > 40) { //Health insurance not allowed for
person above 60 age and term period greater than 40 years
            return false;
        }else{
            return true;
        }
    }
}

contract GeneralAgent is HealthInsuranceAgent {
    //Define mapping to store key-value pairs
    mapping(string => userRecord) userRecordMapping;

    //Organize user records using struct
    struct userRecord
    {
        string unique_identification;
        string name;
        int age;
        bool is_smoke;
        bool is_consume_alcohol;
        int time_period;
        bool has_health_insurance;
        int health_insurance_amount;
    }
    //Save user record. Test data to test on Remix -
("U123",20,"Jon",true,true,10,false,0)
    function saveUserDetails(string memory unique_identification, int age,
string memory name, bool is_smoke, bool is_consume_alcohol, int time_
period, bool has_health_insurance, int health_insurance_amount) public
    {
```

```
        userRecordMapping[unique_identification] = userRecord(unique_
identification, name, age, is_smoke, is_consume_alcohol, time_period,
has_health_insurance, health_insurance_amount);
    }


    //Performs health insurance for given user. Test data to test on Remix -
("U123")
        function doHealthInsurance(string memory unique_identification)
public payable returns (bool) {
        if(checkEligibility(userRecordMapping[unique_identification].age,
userRecordMapping[unique_identification].time_period)){ //Function
from parent contract
        //Function from parent contract
        int insurance_amount =
insuranceAmountCalculator(userRecordMapping[unique_
identification].age,userRecordMapping[unique_identification].
is_smoke, userRecordMapping[unique_identification].is_consume_
alcohol,userRecordMapping[unique_identification].time_period);
        require(insurance_amount > 0); //Furnish positive numbers only
            userRecordMapping[unique_identification].health_insurance_
amount = insurance_amount;
            userRecordMapping[unique_identification].has_health_insurance
= true;
        return true;
    }else{
        return false;
    }
}
    //Get user health insurance details - Test data to test on Remix - ("U123")
    function getUserDetails(string memory unique_identification) public
view returns(bool has_health_insurance, int health_insurance_amount){
        return (userRecordMapping[unique_identification].has_health_
insurance, userRecordMapping[unique_identification].health_insurance_
amount);
    }
}
```

2. **Multilevel Inheritance:** Recipe that will help you understand interface approach for multilevel inheritance

```
pragma solidity ^0.5.1;

/**
 * @title Insurance interface
 */
interface IInsurance {
    function approveInsurance(bytes32 policyId, address sender) external
returns (bool);
    function calculatePremium() external pure returns (string memory);
        //   function   registerClaim(bytes32   policyId,   bytes32
coverageCondition,address reporter) external returns (bool);
        // function claimRelease(bytes32 policyId, address sender) external
returns (bool);


    event Approval(address indexed owner,bytes32 policyId);
}
```

3. **Multiple Inheritance:** "multi_inheritance.sol" - Recipe to comprehend multiple inheritance.

```
pragma solidity ^0.5.1;

import "./insurance_company.sol";
import "./Ownable.sol";

/*
Import statement for Ownable.sol contract is from open source code source
openzeppelin-solidity.
```

```
You need to create a file with name "Ownable.sol" in this chapter's
main folder by copying code from https://github.com/OpenZeppelin/
openzeppelin-solidity/blob/master/contracts/ownership/Ownable.sol
*/
contract companyA is InsuranceCompany, Ownable {

    function calculatePremium() external pure returns (string memory){
        return "calculate from companyA contract";
    }
}
```

4. **Hierarchical Inheritance: "hierarchical_inheritance.sol"** - To create recipe to understand solidity hierarchical inheritance, paste following code snippet into this file.

```
pragma solidity ^0.5.1;

import "./insurance_company.sol";
import "./Ownable.sol";

/*
Import statement for Ownable.sol contract is from opensource code source
openzeppelin-solidity
You need to create a file with name "Ownable.sol" in same folder by copying
code from https://github.com/OpenZeppelin/openzeppelin-solidity/blob/
master/contracts/ownership/Ownable.sol
*/
contract companyB is InsuranceCompany, Ownable {

    function calculatePremium() external pure returns (string memory){
        return "calculate from companyA contract";
    }
}
```

Note - The import statement for Ownable.sol contract is from open source openzeppelin-solidity

5. You need to create a file with name "Ownable.sol" in same folder by copying code from https://github.com/OpenZeppelin/ openzeppelin-solidity/blob/master/contracts/ownership/ Ownable.sol

```
contract companyB is InsuranceCompany, Ownable {
function calculatePremium() external pure returns (string memory){
return "calculate from companyA contract";
}
}
```

6. Run on Remix Online Editor: As we discussed earlier, solidity embeds entire parent (base) contract bytecode into child (derived) contract and generates a single unified contract. As a result, we need to deploy only the single child contract.

For example, to deploy contract "health_insurance_company.sol" on Remix, please follow the following steps:

1. Open https://remix.ethereum.org.

2. Create following files on Remix with code snippet mentioned above. **interface_insurance.sol, insurance_company.sol** and **health_insurance_company.sol**

3. Inside 'Run', choose environment in the dropdown to 'JavaScript VM'.

4. As a next step, choose "companyA" contract from dropdown and deploy it. After the deployment, test the function with test data provided in recipe code. See consolidated steps in the screenshot below to connect all the dots:

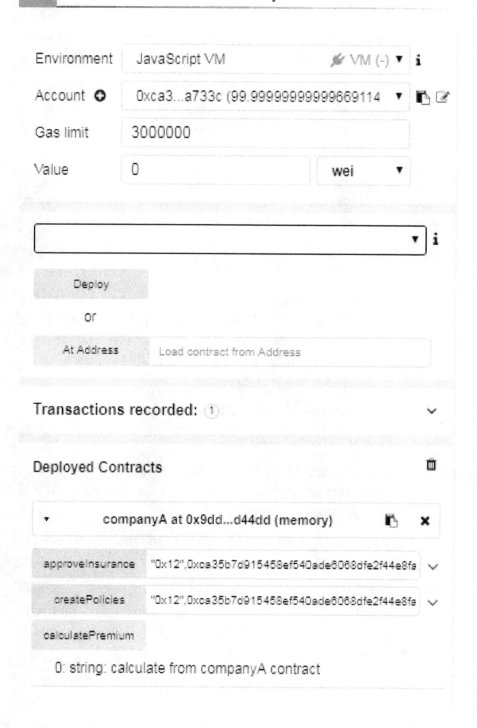

Solidity follows inheritance tree to achieve multi-level inheritance. The best practice for achieving multi-level inheritance in solidity is interface approach. This requires an out-of-the-box manifestation of the concept. Let us draw an inheritance tree for our insurance contracts

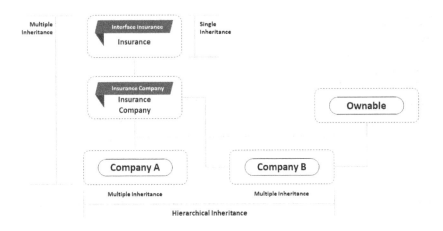

In Solidity, contract hierarchy tree usually keeps interface contract as root contract. This is the real essence behind calling it an interface approach.

There is a fundamental reason for keeping interface as root contract. Essentially a contract does not implement the method inside the contract. This rather keeps all methods with name and arguments' details that derived contract has to implement. Derived contract is forced to have all functions from interface with definition, else it will not be deployed. We will discuss this scenario with a crisp and concise recipe in Remix in the next topic within this chapter.

Ideally, by having interface contract as root contract we can set compliance for our hierarchical inheritance tree.

As we depicted in the image above, our "InsuranceCompany" contract is inheriting interface contract 'Insurance' in order to achieve "Single Inheritance".

> InsuranceCompany is Insurance

"CompanyA" contract inheriting "InsuranceCompany" to achieve multilevel inheritance.

> CompanyA is InsuranceCompany is Insurance

"CompanyA" contract inheriting "InsuranceCompany" and "Ownable" contract to achieve multiple inheritance.

> CompanyA is InsuranceCompany, Ownable

And, "CompanyA" and "CompanyB" both inherit "InsuranceCompany" and "Ownable" contract to achieve hierarchical inheritance.

> CompanyA is InsuranceCompany, Ownable
> CompanyB is InsuranceCompany, Ownable

We will discuss Interfaces in detail in next topic within this chapter.

Additional Context

In inheritance, tree solidity achieves encapsulation using its visibility modifiers i.e private, public, external and internal. Solidity also supports polymorphism along with function overriding and overloading. In our insurance example, you will see following method overridden that will provide you some food for thought.

> function calculatePremium() external pure returns (string memory){}

Abstract and Interface Contracts

If you are familiar with programming languages having object oriented roots then you will know that when a class is declared with keyword "abstract", it becomes abstract even if it may or may not have any abstract method. Solidity on the other hand follows different approach to accomplish this as there is no keyword 'abstract' to define contract as abstract. A contract becomes abstract automatically when it has one or more functions that has missing implementations. Abstract is just virtual concept in solidity and works indirectly.

Abstract contracts cannot be instantiated but can be used as parent contract similar to the concept of interfaces. Solidity provides 'interface' keywords to define a contract as an interface. It does not authorize definition of functions inside it. It keeps all methods with name and arguments details that derived contract has to implement. Derived contract is forced to have all functions from interface with definition. If this is not achieved, it will not get deployed. Like abstract contracts, interfaces cannot be instantiated.

Let's learn the concepts with the recipes show-cased in the upcoming section.

Pre Deep Dive Considerations

Firstly, launch the VS code editor to write and edit code blocks. We begin by creating a folder named 'solidity_programming_practical_samples'. In the browser, open the Remix online editor to compile and run the recipe code blocks.

Code Recipes for Practical Learning

1. Create the following files in VScode, "abstract.sol" - To create recipe to understand solidity abstract contract, paste the following code snippet in this file. Let us convert our "insurance_company.sol" contract to abstract by uncommenting following two lines.

```
// function registerClaim(bytes32 policyId, bytes32
coverageCondition,address reporter) external returns (bool);
// function claimRelease(bytes32 policyId, address sender) external
returns (bool);
```

Now the contract looks like this:

```solidity
pragma solidity ^0.5.1; /**
* @Title Insurance Contract */
import "./interface_insurance.sol";
contract InsuranceCompany is Insurance{
mapping(address => bytes32) createdPolicies; //Create dummy policies
Use test data as ("0x12",0xca35b7d915458ef540ade6068dfe2f44e8fa733c)
function createPolicies(bytes32 policyId, address sender) external {
createdPolicies[sender] = policyId;
}
//Approve policies. Use test data as
("0x12",0xca35b7d915458ef540ade6068dfe2f44e8fa733c)
function approveInsurance(bytes32 policyId, address sender) external
returns (bool){
_approveInsurance(policyId,sender); return true;
}
function calculatePremium() external pure returns (string memory){
return "calculate from Insurance contract";
}
function registerClaim(bytes32 policyId,bytes32 coverageCondition,address
reporter) external returns (bool);
function claimRelease(bytes32 policyId, address sender) external returns
(bool); event Approval(address indexed owner);
function _approveInsurance(bytes32 policyId, address sender) internal
returns (bool)
{
require(createdPolicies[sender] == policyId); emit Approval(sender,
policyId);
}}
```

"interface.sol" - Create recipe to understand solidity interface in solidity.
Let's use our insurance interface once again to demonstrate it.

```solidity
pragma solidity ^0.5.1; /*
* @title Insurance interface
```

```
*/
interface Insurance {
function approveInsurance() external returns (bool);
function calculatePremium() external pure returns (string memory);
function registerClaim() external returns (bool);
function claimRelease() external returns (bool);
}
```

2. Perform the following on the Remix Online Editor:

   1. Open https://remix.ethereum.org.
   2. Create following files on Remix with code mentioned above.
   3. Inside 'Run', choose environment in the dropdown called 'JavaScript VM'.
   4. You will get following error when you try to deploy any of the above contracts:

Interface allows other contracts to inherit it as parent contract. Interface ensures that all contracts that implement it should behave similarly i.e child contracts must implement all methods available in interface otherwise solidity does not allow its deployment on EVM.

To corroborate this submission, let's create a contract file "test_interface.sol" and countenance it to implement "interface.sol". In "test_interface.sol", we have implemented only one method from "interface.sol".

On Remix, create following two files with mentioned code snippet:

"test_interface.sol"

```
pragma solidity ^0.5.1; import "./interface.sol"; /**
* @Title Insurance interface */
contract Insurance is Insurance {
function approveInsurance() external returns (bool){ return true;
}
}
```

"interface.sol".

```
pragma solidity ^0.5.1; /**
* @Title Insurance interface */
interface Insurance {
function approveInsurance() external returns (bool);
function calculatePremium() external pure returns (string memory);
function registerClaim() external returns (bool);
function claimRelease() external returns (bool); }
```

Now try to deploy "test_interface.sol" on remix. You will get an error similar to below depiction:

This contract does not implement all functions and thus cannot be created.

OK

Reason : "test_interface.sol" contract has three more methods that are not implemented yet in conjunction with its parent "interface.sol".

The abstract contract also functions similar to an interface, except below:

- It supports the implementation of functions unlike interface.

- By implementing function behavior, it forces its child contract to keep it's behavior same as the parent function. Interface gives freedom to sub contracts to implement any function unconditionally hence provides flexibility. This makes overall approach user friendly as readers have more control on the business logic implementation.

Additional Context

Best practice when implementing multilevel inheritance in solidity is to use interface as super parent class. By doing this, we provide freedom to derived classes to implement function in customized modus by abiding interface rules.

Special Mention: OpenZeppelin uses similar concept to create ERC20 standard tokens.

Events in Solidity

Solidity events create logs on EVM. From solidity code, we execute events with parameters. They in turn circle back to client while logging provenance to blockchain. Events are inheritable from parent to child. They are used in diverse scenarios. Let's get our hands dirty and learn the concepts with recipes show-cased in the upcoming section.

Pre Deep Dive Considerations

First and foremost, launch the VS code editor to write and edit code. We begin by creating a folder named 'solidity_programming_practical_samples'. On the browser, open the Remix online editor to compile and run the recipe code.

Code Recipes for Practical Learning

1. Create following files in VScode, "abstract_test_event.sol" - create abstract contract recipe to understand event inheritance. Paste following code snippet in this file.

```
pragma solidity ^0.5.1; /**
* @Title Insurance interface */
//This interface has only one function and event

contract IInsurance {
function approveInsurance(bytes32 policyId, address sender) external
returns (bool);
event Approval(address indexed owner,bytes32 policyId); //Event to log
note post approval
```

```
}
//"test_event.sol" - To create recipe to understand solidity events. Paste
following code snippet in this file.

pragma solidity ^0.5.1;
import "./interface_test_event.sol"; /**
* @Title Insurance interface */
contract InsuranceCompany is Insurance { mapping(address => bytes32)
createdPolicies;

//create dummy policies. Test data
-("0x12",0xca35b7d915458ef540ade6068dfe2f44e8fa733c)

function createPolicies(bytes32 policyId, address sender) external {
createdPolicies[sender] = policyId;
}
//Approve policies. Use test data as:
("0x12",0xca35b7d915458ef540ade6068dfe2f44e8fa733c)

function approval(bytes32 policyId, address sender) external returns (bool)
{
_approveInsurance(policyId,sender);
return true;
}

function _approveInsurance(bytes32 policyId, address sender) internal
returns (bool)
{
require(createdPolicies[sender] == policyId);
emit Approval(sender, policyId);
//Emanate Parent interface event
}
}
```

Run on Remix Online Editor:

1. Open https://remix.ethereum.org.
2. Create following files on Remix with code snippet mentioned above.

   Abstract_test_event.sol and test_event.sol

3. Inside 'Run' choose environment in the dropdown to 'JavaScript VM'.

4. Thereafter choose "InsuranceCompany" contract from dropdown and deploy it. After deployment, test the function with test data provided in recipe snippets. See consolidated steps in the screenshot below:

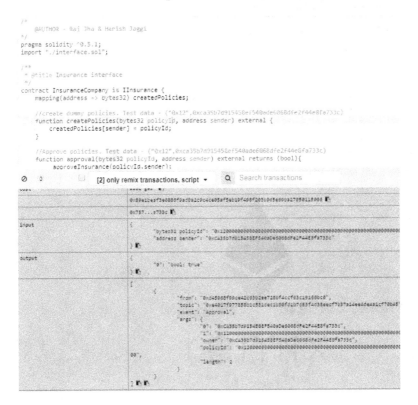

In solidity events are declared using "event" keyword and can be triggered from any function in contract using "emit" keyword. In the event, we can also define the parameters that are required to be emitted. See the following example where we are defining and emitting the event within the same contract. This event will emit message with parameters from_add, to_add, and message_to_send. Try the below-mentioned code snippet on Remix and observe the console log to view the output. Follow "Run on Remix Online Editor" section to successfully execute it on Remix:

```
pragma solidity ^0.5.1; contract SampleEvent {
// SampleEvent : Define event in contract
event message(address from_add, address to_add, string message_to_send);
function sendMessage(address to_add, string memory message_to_send)
public {
// Business logic to send message to append here.
// Event can be triggered by any client such as browser, web3 etc. We have
already seen steps to perform QA on Remix in the previous example.
emit message(msg.sender, to_add, message_to_send); }}
```

Just to re-emphasize, events are inheritable from parent to child. In "Code Recipes for Practical Learning" section we have defined the event in abstract parent class inside "abstract_test_event.sol" as follows:

```
event Approval(address indexed owner,bytes32 policyId); //Event to be
logged post consent.
```

Emit this event in derived contract "test_event.sol" to exhibit inheritance characteristic.

```
emit Approval(sender, policyId); //Emit Parent abstract contract event.
```

Additional Context

We frequently use events to publish logs in our Dapp (Decentralised Application). We will understand and practice Dapp implementation in detail in subsequent chapters. Stay tuned!

Library in Solidity

Library is collection of commonly used code that any contract can re-use. This curtails reinventing the wheel. Library neither has storage nor does it hold ethers (payable and fallback functions are not permissible). With the help of libraries, we avoid repetitive code deployment on blockchain and save gas (ether) used in repetitive code deployment. In solidity library, library{} is defined similar to contract{}. Let's learn the rules of the game with recipes show-cased below.

Pre Deep Dive Considerations

First and foremost, launch the VS code editor to write and edit code. We begin by creating a folder named 'solidity_programming_practical_samples'. On the browser, open the Remix online editor to compile and run the recipe code blocks.

We have used one of the code recipes (value_type_integers_0.sol) that we had developed earlier to show insecure integer overflow by giving it an interesting variation.

Code Recipes for Practical Learning

1. We have insecure code where balances[msg.sender] i.e. _ value >= 0 condition always gets gratified as uint minus uint operation always returns uint and uint is always greater or equal to 0. Hence, check in transfer() function always returns true. Allowing senders to transfer amount greater than what they actually possess can create havoc.

2. In this example, the sender has initial balance of 100 ethers, i.e. balanceOf[msg.sender] = 100. While executing transfer function, we are transferring 200 ethers i.e. (0xca35b7d915458ef540ade6068dfe2f44e8fa733c,200)

```
pragma solidity ^0.5.1; contract InsecureIntegerFlow{
mapping (address => uint256) public balanceOf;
function transfer(address _to, uint256 _value) public {
(0xca35b7d915458ef540ade6068dfe2f44e8fa733c,200) on remix.
balanceOf[msg.sender] = 100; //Set balance of address to 100.
/* Check if sender has balance as this can potentially cause integer
overflow. balances[msg.sender] - _value >= 0 condition is always satisfied
because uint minus uint operation always renders uint and uint is always
greater or equal to 0.
We have set sender address balance to 100. We need to check that transfer
occurs only when the sender has sufficient balance to send money, i.e.
balanceOf[msg.sender] - _value >= 0. Due to integer overflow reasons
```

```
explained above, the condition balanceOf[msg.sender] - _value >= 0 is
always true. Thus, the sender can transfer any amount to the destination
address.*/

require(balanceOf[msg.sender] - _value >= 0);
//This line of code can create disaster.
/* Add and subtract new balances */
balanceOf[msg.sender] -= _value; balanceOf[_to] += _value;
}
}
```

To solve this problem, we are using the open source Safemath library
provided by OpenZeppelin. We are using this library since this is tried
and tested against umpteen number of security standards and is being
used by several blockchain projects across the globe. Let's do some
changes in our code snippet to make our transfer() function secure.
Let's create our solution contract file with the name "library_solution_
uint.sol" in VScode and paste the following code snippet in this file.

```
"./SafeMath.sol";

contract secureIntegerFlow{
//Change name from Insecure to Secure as we have implemented SafeMath
mapping (address => uint256) public balanceOf;
function transfer(address _to, uint256 _value) public {
(0xca35b7d915458ef540ade6068dfe2f44e8fa733c,200) on remix.
balanceOf[msg.sender] = 100;
//Set balance address to 100.
/* Check if sender has balance as this can potentially cause integer
overflow. balances[msg.sender] - _value >= 0 condition is always satisfied
because uint minus uint operation always renders uint and uint is always
greater or equal to 0.
We have set sender address balance to 100. We need to check that transfer
occurs only when the sender has sufficient balance to send money, i.e.
```

```
balanceOf[msg.sender] - _value >= 0. Due to integer overflow reasons
explained above, condition balanceOf[msg.sender] - _value >= 0 is always
true. Thus sender can transfer any amount to the destination address.*/ //
require(balanceOf[msg.sender] - _value >= 0);
//This line of code can create disaster.
require(SafeMath.sub(balanceOf[msg.sender],_value) >= 0);
//There is protection in place now using SafeMath Lib.
/* Add and subtract new balances */
balanceOf[msg.sender] -= _value;
balanceOf[_to] += _value;
}
}
```

Create SafeMath.sol file to keep SafeMath code match solidity compiler version. Copy Safemath contract code directly from https://github.com/OpenZeppelin/openzeppelin-solidity/blob/master/contracts/math/SafeMath.sol

Please change pragma version to pragma solidity ^0.5.1.

3. Run on Remix Online Editor:

1. Open https://remix.ethereum.org.
2. Create following files on Remix with code snippet mentioned above.
3. library_solution_uint.sol and SafeMath.sol
4. Inside 'Run', choose environment in the dropdown to 'JavaScript VM'.
5. Thereafter choose "secureIntegerFlow" contract from dropdown and deploy it. After deployment, test the function with test data provided in recipe snippets. See consolidated steps in the screenshot below:

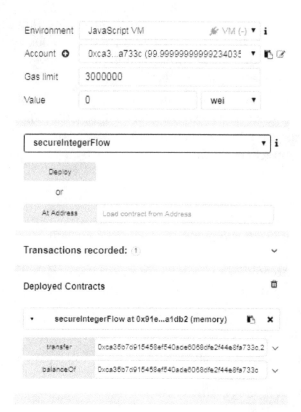

5. When readers try to execute transfer() function with amount greater than 100 (actual balance of sender) then it should provide VM error as depicted below in Remix console:

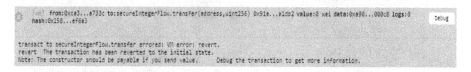

In library_solution_uint.sol contract, we have imported SafeMath library.

```
import "./SafeMath.sol";
```

Calling its method SafeMath.sub() to subtract uint from uint is the key.

SafeMath sub() function will throw VM error if we try to perform uint underflow or overflow.

```
require(SafeMath.sub(balanceOf[msg.sender],_value) >= 0); //This line of
code is providing much needed protection using SafeMath Lib.
```

Additional Context

When any contract calls functions from library, it gets compiled as 'DELEGATECALL'. This ensures library code should execute within the context of contract been called. Sender contract sends 'DELEGATECALL' to receiver's library and allows the receiver to use its storage thereby performing operation based on business logic. This kind of freedom is vulnerable being potential security risk for the sender contract as it shares its storage to untrusted contract/library to execute it's code. We will discuss this in detail while discussing opcodes and security considerations in later part of this book.

Global Variables in Solidity

After deployment, contracts gets live on blockchain and allows external entities to interact with it via approved transactions. In some scenarios external entities need to get current states of blockchain through contract methods. Good news is Ethereum provides some global variables that contracts can trust to get current state of blockchain. Contracts can realize blockchain states related to block, transaction, message, account and address. Let's see this in action in the next section.

Pre Deep Dive Considerations

First and foremost, launch the VS code editor to write and edit code blocks. We begin by creating a folder named 'solidity_programming_practical_samples'. On the browser, open the Remix online editor to compile and run the recipe code.

Code Recipes for Practical Learning

1. Create solidity contract with name "global_variables.sol" to test all global variables available in ethereum blockchain that readers can call using solidity code. Paste the following code snippet in this file.

```
pragma solidity ^0.5.1; contract globalVariables{
function getBlockRelatedGlobalVariables() public view
returns (address,uint,uint,uint,bytes32,uint){
/*
block.coinbase – Get miner address for current block. block.difficulty – Find
difficulty of current block. block.gaslimit – Get gaslimit of current block.
block.number – Find number of current block. block.blockhash – Retrieve
hash of block.
block.timestamp – Ascertain timestamp of current block.
*/

bytes32 blockchash = blockhash(block.number);
return (block.coinbase, block.difficulty, block.gaslimit, block.number,
blockchash, block.timestamp);
}
function getMessageRelatedGlobalVariables() public payable
returns (bytes memory,uint, address, uint){
//See output on Remix console
/*
msg.data – calldata (complete)
gasleft – Depicts Remaining Gas. In previous versions, it was msg.gas.
msg. sender – Sender of message.
msg.value – No. of wei sent with message.
*/
uint gas_left = gasleft();
return (msg.data, gas_left, msg.sender, msg.value);
//See output on Remix console}
function getTxRelatedGlobalVariables() public view
returns (uint, address){
```

```
/*
tx.gasprice - Transaction's gas price.
tx.origin - message sender (full call chain)
*/
return (tx.gasprice, tx.origin);
//Get miner address for current block.
}
function getOtherGlobalVariables() public view
returns (uint, uint){
/*
address(this).balance – Renders balance of current contract. addr.balance –
Renders balance of given ethereum account(addr).
*/
return (address(this).balance, msg.sender.balance);
//Render miner's address for current block.
}
}
```

2. Run on Remix Online Editor:

   1. Open https://remix.ethereum.org.
   2. Create following files on Remix with code snippet mentioned above.
      Global_variables.sol
   3. Inside 'Run', choose environment in the dropdown to 'JavaScript VM'.
   4. Then choose "globalVariables" contract from dropdown and deploy it. After deployment, test the function. See consolidated steps in the screenshot below:

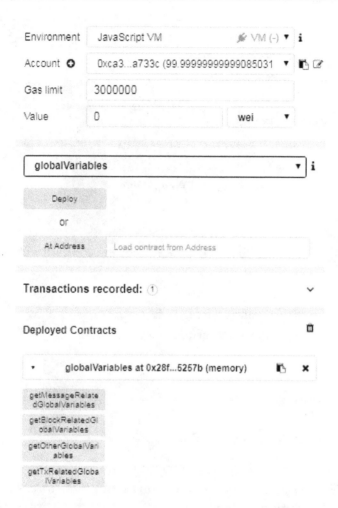

Global variables provide correct and current blockchain state. On blockchain these global variables are managed based on underneath consensus mechanism. Below is the mapping of global variables and corresponding state it returns to contract.

Block Related Global Variables

These global variables are used to detect state of current block. It shares details such as miner address, difficulty level, gas limit, count, hash and timestamp for current block.

block.coinbase	Miner address for current block
block.difficulty	Difficulty of current block
block.gaslimit	Gas limit of current block
block.number	Number of current block
block.blockhash	Hash of block
block.timestamp	Timestamp of current block

Message Related Global Variables

These global variables are used to detect current state from blockchain. It helps with information such as calldata, remaining gas, address of message sender and value (in wei) sent with message

msg.data	Call information
gasleft	Gas remaining
msg.sender	Sender of message
msg.value	No. of wei being exchanged

Transaction Related Global Variables

These global variables are used to detect current state of transaction. It helps with information such as gas price coupled with complete chain of transaction to detect origin.

tx.gasprice	Transaction's gas price
tx.origin	Message sender (full chain)

Account and Address Related Global Variables

These global variables are used to detect address properties. It helps with information such as balance of current contract and given account.

address(this).balance	Balance of current contract
addr.balance	Renders balance of given ethereum account

Additional Context

We already have used few of these global variables in our recipes. We will use others in the subsequent chapters as we write complex recipes.

Solidity Assembly

Solidity is a high-level language that uses solidity compiler for assembly conversion to interact with EVM. It provides a way to entrench assembly code directly in Solidity code thereby making it unique and impactful. This enables capability in contracts to directly interact with EVM using opcode to perform complex tasks with much better control and ease. Assembly code is not always safe because it abandons solidity compiler's security checks. We can also write assembly code in a standalone mode without using inline snippets in solidity code. Understanding assembly in solidity is cumbersome and compound hence out of the scope of this book. In this book, we are demonstrating the ways we can develop solutions by embedding (inline) assembly code in Solidity contracts. Let's get on a roll to explore concepts using crisp recipes.

Pre Deep Dive Considerations

First and foremost, launch the VS code editor to write and edit code blocks. We begin by creating a folder named 'solidity_programming_practical_samples'. On the browser, open the Remix online editor to compile and run the recipe code blocks.

Please open code recipe "value_type_string_byte.sol" we had developed earlier for your ready reference.

Code Recipes for Practical Learning

1. We use assembly code when solidity code is not optimized to perform a task. One such example is as below:

```
pragma solidity ^0.5.1;
contract StringLessthen32CharecterToByte32 {
//Conversion of string less than 32 characters long to bytes32
function toBytes32(string memory _string) public pure returns (bytes32) {
//Try argument ("Rendezvous with Practical Solidity")
//Pure means we are neither accessing state nor changing state
//Make sure string should be of less than 32 characters
require(bytes(_string).length <= 32); bytes32 _stringBytes;
//This is recommended way of conversion from string to bytes32 assembly
{
//Assembly block to embed assembly code
//32 passes over non-core data parts of string
_stringBytes := mload(add(_ string, 32))
//Using "add" opcode to load the memory pointer.
}
return _stringBytes;
}
}
```

2. Another pertinent opportunity to use assembly inline code is where solidity itself is not capable of performing tasks such as 'contract not able to read another external contract'. See code recipe below to understand it better. Real essence is to use library to render external contract code and store it in bytes array.

3. Please create a new file in VScode and name it "assembly_ example.sol". Paste the following code in file.

```
pragma solidity ^0.5.1;
//Library to get external contract code and store it in bytes outputByteArray
library ReadAnotherContractCode {
function contract_at(address externalCodeAddress) public view returns (bytes
memory outputByteArray) {
assembly {
let extCodeSize := extcodesize(externalCodeAddress)
//Read code size of external contract
outputByteArray := mload(0x40)
//Output-byte-array allocation. 0x40 is free memory pointer where memory
can be used
mstore(0x40, add(outputByteArray, and(add(add(extCodeSize, 32), 0x1f),
not(0x1f))))
//Find end of memory pointer including padding mstore(outputByteArray,
extCodeSize)
//Ascertain length of store in memory
extcodecopy(externalCodeAddress, add(outputByteArray, 32), 0, extCodeSize)
//Render external contract code
    }
  }
}
```

Note - Please ponder over comments in recipe code file to understand each line of code in depth.

    4. Run on Remix Online Editor:

        1. Open https://remix.ethereum.org.

        2. Create following files on Remix with code snippet mentioned above.

           Assembly_example.sol

    5. Inside 'Run' choose environment in the dropdown to 'JavaScript VM'.

    6. Then choose "ReadAnotherContractCode" contract from dropdown and deploy it. After deployment, test the function "contract_at". Pass any other deployed contract address as argument of "contract_at" method. See consolidated steps in the screenshot below:

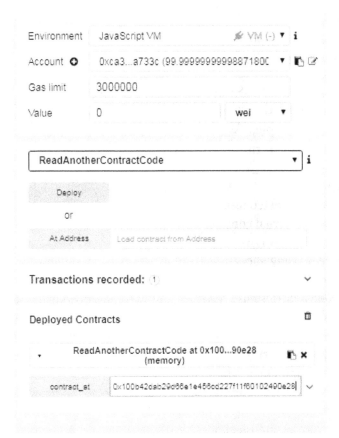

Assembly {} block is used to write assembly code in solidity. Local variables within scope of assembly block can be created using "let" keyword.

```
assembly {
let extCodeSize := extcodesize(externalCodeAddress) }
```

Assembly uses "free memory pointer" at location of "0x40" to manage memory location. For memory allocation it considers current position of "free memory pointer" i..e "0x40" and commences allocating memory thereafter.

```
pos := mload(0x40) //Find free memory pointer positionmstore(0x40,
add(pos, length)) //Start memory allocation from the pointer till end of
data
```

That being said, it uses 64 bytes of memory as scratch space. 32 bytes after "0x40" i.e "0x60" is mapped to 0. In reality actually allocated memory starts from "0x80".

Assembly block uses opcodes to perform operations on EVM. We have used opcodes like extcodesize, mload, add, mstore and extcodecopy in our recipe examples. We will see all prominent opcodes in detail in subsequent topics of this chapter.

```
assembly {
let extCodeSize := extcodesize(externalCodeAddress)
//Read size of external contract.
outputByteArray := mload(0x40)
//Output-byte-array allocation. 0x40 is free memory pointer for allocation
and use.
mstore(0x40, add(outputByteArray, and(add(add(extCodeSize, 32), 0x1f),
not(0x1f))))
//Ascertain    end    of    memory    pointer    including    padding.
mstore(outputByteArray, extCodeSize)
//Ascertain length of store in memory.
extcodecopy(externalCodeAddress,    add(outputByteArray,    32),    0,
extCodeSize)
//Render external contract code
}
```

Additional Context

There are ways to assign external variables and implement if, loop, switch, statements and function calls in assembly block. Please practice these in recipes and learn the rules.

Using For Declarations

In solidity, 'using' keyword is to include a solidity library within a solidity contract. In addition, 'for' keyword indicate possible types for which library has been included. These are important concepts to understand. Let's ponder over various recipes showcased in the upcoming section and get a deep understanding of the concepts.

Consider the following example:

```
using extLibrary for uint;
//include library for uint datatype.
using extLibrary for *;
//include library for any datatype.
```

Pre Deep Dive Considerations

First and foremost, launch the VS code editor to write and edit code blocks. We begin by creating a folder called 'solidity_programming_practical_samples'. On the browser, open the Remix online editor to compile and run the recipe code blocks.

Code Recipes for Practical Learning

1. Create the following files in VScode "using_for_example1. sol" - To create recipe to understand how we can use a solidity library in a solidity contract for certain datatype. Paste the following code snippet in this file:

```
pragma solidity ^0.5.1;
library myLibraryForCalculations {
/* @Dev Safe subtraction between two uint */
function sub(uint256 one, uint256 two) internal pure returns (uint256) {
require(two <= one);
uint256 tmp = one - two; return tmp;
}
/* @dev Safe addition between two uint */
function add(uint256 one, uint256 two) internal pure returns (uint256) {
  uint256 tmp = one + two;
require(tmp >= one); return tmp;
}
}
contract calculator{
using myLibraryForCalculations for uint;
//Include library for uint datatype
function add_numbers(uint a, uint b) public pure returns (uint){
return a.add(b);
```

```
//Declaration allows syntactic sugar syntax such as a.add(b);
}
function substract_numbers(uint a, uint b) public pure returns (uint){
return a.sub(b);
//Declaration allows syntactic sugar syntax such ss a.sub(b);
}
}
contract calculator1{
function add_numbers(uint a, uint b) public pure returns (uint){
return myLibraryForCalculations.add(a,b);
//Case of not using "using for" declaration
}
function substract_numbers(uint a, uint b) public pure returns (uint){
return myLibraryForCalculations.sub(a,b);
//Case of not using "using for" declaration
}
} //Case of not using "using for" declaration }
}
```

2. "using_for_example2.sol" – Goal of this recipe is to demonstrate use of solidity library in a solidity contract for any datatype. Paste the following code snippet in this file.

```
/*
pragma solidity ^0.5.1;
library myLibraryForCalculations {
/* @Dev safe subtraction between two uint. */
function sub(uint256 one, uint256 two) internal pure returns (uint256) {
require(two <= one);
uint256 tmp = one - two; return tmp;
}
/* @Dev safe addition between two uint. */
function add(uint256 one, uint256 two) internal pure returns (uint256) {
uint256 tmp = one + two;
require(tmp >= one); return tmp;
}
```

```solidity
/* @Dev check */
function compare(uint256 one, uint256 two) internal pure returns (bool) {
if(one > two){
//Ascertain if one is greater than two
return true;
}
else{
return false;
}
}
}
contract calculator{
//Using myLibraryForCalculations for *; Include library for any datatype.
function add_numbers(uint a, uint b) public pure returns (uint){
return a.add(b);
//Declaration allows syntactic sugar syntax such as a.add(b);
}
function substract_numbers(uint a, uint b) public pure returns (uint){
return a.sub(b);
//Declaration allows syntactic sugar syntax such as a.sub(b);
}
function compare_number(uint a, uint b) public pure returns (bool){
return a.compare(b);
//Using-for declaration allows to use syntactic sugar syntax such as a.sub(b);
}
}
contract calculator1{
function add_numbers(uint a, uint b) public pure returns (uint){
return myLibraryForCalculations.add(a,b);
//Case of not using "using for" declaration
}
function substract_numbers(uint a, uint b) public pure returns (uint){
return myLibraryForCalculations.sub(a,b);
//Case of not using "using for" declaration
}
```

```
function compare_number(uint a, uint b) public pure returns (bool){
return myLibraryForCalculations.compare(a,b);
//Case of not using "using for" declaration
}
}
```

3. Run on Remix Online Editor:

   1. Open https://remix.ethereum.org.
   2. Create following files on Remix with code provided above. using_for_example1.sol and using_for_example2.sol

4. Inside 'Run' choose environment in the dropdown to 'JavaScript VM'.

5. Then choose "calculator" contract from dropdown and deploy it. After deployment, test the functions. See consolidated steps in the screenshot below for using_for_example1.sol contract.

In contract "using_for_example1.sol", below line in "contract calculator{}" enables rendering library for uint datatype.

> using myLibraryForCalculations for uint; //Include library for uint datatype

It means any uint datatype can use library function using syntactically sugar syntax i.e

> return a.add(b); //Declaration allows to use syntactic sugar syntax like a.add(b);

If we make "using myLibraryForCalculations for uint;" redundant from "contract calculator{}" as done in "contract calculator1{}", we have to use the library function as given below: "myLibraryForCalculations. add(a,b);"

Reason: This will not allow readers to use library functions anymore with syntactically sugar syntax:

```
contract calculator1{
function add_numbers(uint a, uint b) public pure returns (uint){
return myLibraryForCalculations.add(a,b);
//Case of not using "using for" declaration
}
function substract_numbers(uint a, uint b) public pure returns (uint){
return myLibraryForCalculations.sub(a,b);
//Case of not using "using for" declaration
}
}
```

In contract "using_for_example2.sol", we have demonstrated rendering library in contracts to allow many datatypes using the following line:

> using myLibraryForCalculations for *; //Render library for any datatype.
>
> Refer to "contract calculator{}" where we have used library function for uint and bool both.
>
> contract calculator{

```
using myLibraryForCalculations for *;
//Include library for any datatype
function add_numbers(uint a, uint b) public pure returns (uint){
return a.add(b);
//Declaration allows to use syntactic sugar syntax such as a.add(b);
}
function substract_numbers(uint a, uint b) public pure returns (uint){
return a.sub(b);
//Declaration allows to use syntactic sugar syntax such as a.sub(b);
}
function compare_number(uint a, uint b) public pure returns (bool){
return a.compare(b);
//Declaration allows to use syntactic sugar syntax such as a.sub(b);
}
}
```

Also in "contract calculator1{}", we demonstrated library function render procedure for multiple datatypes if we are not using "using myLibraryForCalculations for *;" declaration.

Additional Context

Using-for declaration also works in case of struct and array. We have developed a crisp recipe to demonstrate the use of 'Using-for' declaration with Struct data structure below.

```
pragma solidity ^0.5.1; library structLib {
struct Container {
mapping(uint => bool) items;
}
//struct example
function insert(Container storage self, uint value) public returns (bool)
{
if (self.items[value]) return false;
self.items[value] = true;
```

```solidity
//Insert in struct and return true.
return true;
}
function contains(Container storage self, uint value) public view returns
(bool) {
return self.items[value];
//Ascertain item in items list
}
}
contract structOperations{
using structLib for structLib.Container;
//Struct example
structLib.Container items;
//Make as struct
//Test-data - (80)
function pushItems(uint value) public {
require(items.insert(value));
//Insert in struct
}
//Test-data - (80)
function checkItems(uint value) public view returns (bool) {
return items. contains(value); /
/Ascertain item in items.
}
}
```

Output snapshot from Remix for your reference:

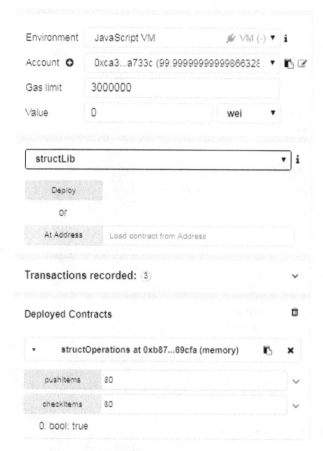

Payable and Withdrawal

Payable is a modifier in solidity that we have briefly comprehended in previous topics. Payable allows methods to receive funds in ethers. One contract can have multiple functions with payable modifier to perform multiple and diverse tasks. To transfer ethers, solidity suggests to use withdraw pattern where contract does not push fund to recipient address. Mechanism rather allows recipients to retrieve funds from contract. This is accomplished to mitigate security risks that can manifest in case of failed external calls. Some of the examples of external call failure while transferring funds to recipient addresses are:

- If recipient (receiver) address is a malicious contract. In this case, it might have fallback function that can throw exception when get triggered.

- Running out of gas when the same function is trying to push funds to multiple addresses.

Pre Deep Dive Considerations

First and foremost, launch the VS code editor to write and edit code blocks. We begin by creating a folder called 'solidity_programming_practical_samples'. On the browser, open the Remix online editor to compile and run the recipe code blocks.

Code Recipes for Practical Learning

1. Create following files in VScode, "payable_transfer.sol" to write the recipe to demonstrate the push transfer example. In this file, we have three contracts "myGame", "Player1" and "Player2". Paste the following code snippet in this file.

```
pragma solidity ^0.5.1;
contract myGame {
uint fixhighestScore = 100;
//Highest score is 100
constructor () public payable{}
//Payable constructor
function play(uint score, address payable contractAddr) external payable {
//External play function
if(score >= fixhighestScore){ contractAddr.transfer(msg.value);
/* Transfer to Player1 contract address. Play halts if this external call fails.
*/
}
}
function chkBalanceOfAccount() public view returns (uint256){ //Get
balance of account that is used to execute contract on Remix.
```

```solidity
return msg. sender.balance;
}
function () external payable{
 //Payable fallback function
}
}
contract Player1{
myGame mg;
constructor (address payable _mg) public payable{
//Payable constructor
mg = myGame(_mg);
//Initialize myGame contract inside this contract.
}
function playGame(uint score) public payable {
//Call of function from myGame external contract.
mg.play.value(msg.value)(score,address(this));
}
function chkBalance() public view returns (uint256){
//Ascertain balance of player1 contract
return address(this).balance;
}
function () external payable{
 //Payable fallback function
}
}
contract Player2{ myGame mg;
constructor (address payable _mg) public payable{
//Payable constructor
mg = myGame(_mg);
//Initialize myGame contract inside this contract.
}
//test data - (200)
function playGame(uint score) public payable {
//Invocation of function from myGame external contract.
```

```
mg.play.value(msg.value)(score,address(this));
}
function chkBalance() public view returns (uint256){
//Balance of player1 contract
return address(this).balance
}
function () external payable{
//payable fallback function.
/*
Exemplifies when external call fails due to malicious contract that throws
error in fallback function. As a result, every transfer to this contract will fail
causing loss to account that triggered the transaction.
*/
revert();
}
}
```

2. "payable_withdrawl.sol" demonstrates the pull transfer scenario. In this example, we have two contracts "myGame", "Player1" depicting withdraw pattern. Paste the following code snippet in this file.

Note - Read, "Code Recipes for Practical Learning" section and inline code comments judiciously to successfully execute it on Remix.

3. Run on Remix Online Editor:

   1. Open https://remix.ethereum.org.
   2. Create following files on Remix with code snippet mentioned above.
      Payable_transfer.sol and payable_withdrawl.sol

4. Inside 'Run' choose environment in the dropdown to 'JavaScript VM'.

5. Then choose "myGame" contract from dropdown and deploy it. After deployment, copy address of "myGame" contract.

6. Select "Player1" contract in the dropdown and deploy it using copied address of "myGame".

7. Thereafter execute "playGame" method of "Player1" contract with argument value 200 (Remember - You need to score > 100 to get reward). Reward amount in the recipe is "msg.value" so we have to set this value in Remix to get it as reward. In remix we can set this value in value field. Let's make it 100.

8. This amount is in wei unit and gets awarded to player1 in case of win. You can check the "Player1" account balance using method "chkBalance". Please be sure to double-check 100 wei after "Player1" wins by executing "playGame" method.

9. See consolidated steps in the screenshot below:

Likewise readers can execute contract for "Player2" however you will get error in Remix console.

10. Similarly readers can execute contracts in file "payable_withdrawl.sol". We demonstrated strait and clear that "Player1" needs to pull its reward by making another call. Execution sequence shall be playGame(200) => getRewardAmount() => chkBalance().

11. Executing contract in this file is your homework. For your convenience and ready reference, we are providing Remix consolidated screenshot below:

```
transact to Player2.playGame errored: VM error: revert.
revert  The transaction has been reverted to the initial state.
Note: The constructor should be payable if you send value.    Debug the transaction to get more information.
```

"payable_transfer.sol" has three contracts "myGame", "Player1" and "Player2". "myGame" contract has custom rules. Few important pointers to remember are:

- "myGame" is a contract where we have game rules.

- Any player can play this game. We have created another contract "Player1" to play game.

- If player1 scores more than 100 then he should get a reward equal to the transaction value i.e "msg.value". If player1 scores less than 100, there is however no penalty.

- Contract "myGame" will transfer the reward amount to contract "player1" address each time player1 scores more than 100.

See recipe code judiciously to grasp these business cases in the contracts.

Special Mention: One vital aspect was overlooked in "myGame" contract i.e. pushing the transfer from this contract to player1 contract address. This can introduce vulnerability in contract. In solidity, there is a prominent thumb rule i.e. "one contract should never trust any other contract". Let's look at it once more.

```
function play(uint score, address payable contractAddr) external payable {
//External play function
if(score >= fixhighestScore){
contractAddr.transfer(msg.value);
// Transfer to Player1 contract address. No one else can play if this external
call fails.
}
}
```

So far so good as script got executed between "myGame" and "Player1" according to the business logic. Let's ponder over another scenario. Another player "Player2" has shown keen interest to play "myGame" but unfortunately this "player2" is a malicious contract. He tries to take advantage of "myGame" contract implementation by emulating contract similar to "player1" with one minor twist i.e. exception is thrown in his fallback payable function. When player2 won, "myGame" contract tried to push reward to "Player2" contract but failed due to fallback function 'revert()' method. This caused unnecessary transaction cost to owner of "myGame" and also impacted corresponding code adversely.

Below-mentioned code demonstrates how we can throw error from fallback function in solidity assuming "player2" has implemented payable contract in similar fashion.

```
function () external payable{
//Payable fallback function
/*
Case when external call fails due to malicious contracts who throws error
in fallback function. Due to this, every transfer to this contract will fail and
cause loss to account which triggered the transaction.
*/
revert();
}
```

To resolve this issue, we need to introduce pull reward to reward relevant contracts. Let's ponder over this implementation in "myGame as follows:

```
contract myGame {
----------------------
function play(uint score, address payable contractAddr) external payable {
//External play function
if(score >= fixhighestScore){
//Push transfer and allow recipients to pull using withdrawReward function
rewards[contractAddr] = msg.value;
}
}
function withdrawReward(address payable _toReward) external payable {
//Withdraw function
uint reward = rewards[_toReward];
rewards[_toReward] = 0;
_toReward. transfer(reward);
}
---------------------------
}
contract Player1{
-----------------------------
function getRewardAmount() public payable {
//pull reward amount
mg.withdrawReward.value(msg.value)(address(this));
}
-----------------------------
}
```

Additional Context

Fallback functions enable a contract to accept ether from other contracts or wallets. Other contracts and wallets can send ethers without knowing ABI of the contract to whom they are sending money. One contract can have maximum one fallback function according to the established norm.

Special Mention: Anyone can call fallback function from a contract when:

1. Call for any function that does not exist in contract.

2. Sending ether to contract without any data.

Solidity Bytecode and Opcode

Solidity is high level programming language that is compiled into low-level machine language (bytecode) using solidity compiler that uses EVM (ethereum virtual machine) internally. Bytecode is actually binary string that characterizes hexadecimal format for better representation. Opcodes are instructions to EVM. Each byte-code is 8-bit uint i.e. ADD is 0x01, MUL is 0x02 so on and so forth. Let's pull up our socks and go through with recipes given below.

Pre Deep Dive Considerations

First and foremost, launch the VS code editor to write and edit code blocks. We begin by creating a folder called 'solidity_programming_practical_samples'. On the browser, open the Remix online editor to compile and run the recipe code blocks.

Code Recipes for Practical Learning

1. Let's pick one of the recipe "assembly_example.sol" that we developed in earlier sections of this chapter to comprehend solidity assembly. We have used few opcodes in previous sections to realize external contract code coupled with mechanisms to store it in output-binary-array.

```
pragma solidity ^0.5.1;
//Library to get external contract code and store it in bytes outputByteArray

library ReadAnotherContractCode {
```

```
function contract_at(address externalCodeAddress) public view returns
(bytes memory outputByteArray) {
assembly {
let extCodeSize := extcodesize(externalCodeAddress)
//Read code size of external contract
outputByteArray := mload(0x40)
//Output-byte-array allocation. 0x40 is free memory pointer where 'from
memory' can be used.
mstore(0x40, add(outputByteArray, and(add(add(extCodeSize, 32), 0x1f),
not(0x1f))))
//Ascertain     end     of     memory     pointer     including     padding.
mstore(outputByteArray, extCodeSize)
//Ascertain length of store in memory. extcodecopy(externalCodeAddress,
add(outputByteArray, 32), 0, extCodeSize)
//Render external contract code
}
}
}
```

2. Above recipe will compile into bytecode when we execute it on Remix. Let's understand it in-depth by running it on Remix editor.

3. Run on Remix Online Editor:

   1. Open https://remix.ethereum.org.
   2. Create following files on Remix with code mentioned above.
      Assembly_example.sol
   3. Go to compile tab and compile code on Remix. Thereafter click on "details' button and you will witness bytecode and opcode details as depicted below:

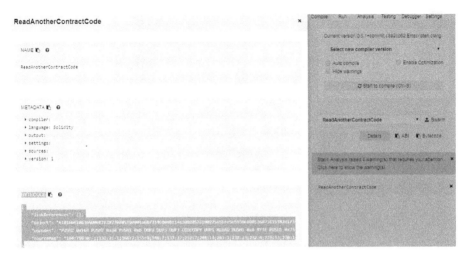

Opcode is a low-level assembly language and is very convoluted to comprehend. Deep-dive is out of the scope for this book hence we provided high level overview for the benefits of readers. We should remember different opcodes, their purpose and hexadecimal equivalents. Being a practical cookbook, we do not want to demonstrate the opcode list for you however, you can directly get yourself enlightened by picking a leaf from various credible sources.

CHAPTER 4

Reviewing Scalability Principles

Introduction

Blockchain network scalability can be measured effectively by the transaction throughput. In this chapter, we will touch upon the strategies on which ethereum core team and its community are working to reduce transaction cost and increase transaction throughput. We will primarily emphasize on Solidity code-scaling strategies like extendibility, upgradability and libraries approaches; which makes code enhancements and extensions easier to execute. On ethereum, every contract deployment and its execution cost gas price so choosing right pattern to scale code is of utmost importance.

Here are the learning outcomes from this chapter:

- Understand smart contract scaling techniques
- Comprehend smart contract upgradeability pattern
- Basic know-how of ethereum network scaling strategies

Technical Requirements

Basic Understanding of Blockchain Basics and Ethereum

- Readers should know and understand basics of blockchain - https://solidity.readthedocs.io/en/latest/introduction-to-smart-contracts.html#blockchain-basics

- Readers should know about ethereum and ethereum virtual machine(EVM) - https://solidity.readthedocs.io/en/latest/introduction-to-smart-contracts.html#index-6

Setup Coding Environment

- Install visual studio code for Windows/Linux/Mac from https://code.visualstudio.com/

- Install Solidity visual studio code extension from visual studio marketplace https://marketplace.visualstudio.com/items?itemName=JuanBlanco.solidity

- Install extension for material icon theme

Implementing Solidity Scaling (upgradeability) Patterns

Introduction

Smart contracts cannot be upgraded or modified once deployed due to immutable nature of ethereum network however in many scenarios, we need our contracts to be modified and prominent scenarios include:

- Update logic in smart contract

- Fix an exploitation done by hackers

- Patch a bug

- Add missing or additional features

- When vulnerabilities need to be fixed due to changes in EVM

- So on and so forth

By using proper techniques and patterns such as proxy contract pattern, data separation technique, delegatecall-based proxies etc, we can make contract logic upgradeable while keeping same storage intact.

Pre Deep Dive Considerations

- Launch VS code editor to write and edit code.

- Create a new folder inside folder 'solidity_programming_ practical_samples' and name it "Reviewing Scalability Principles" if you have not created yet.

- Open Remix online editor on browser to compile and run the recipe code.

Code Recipes for Practical Learning

At the onset - Let's understand one real-world use-case and scenario when we have need to upgrade the contracts. Here is one hypothetical scenario:

There is one insurance company and its software has a business logic that calculates insurance premium for customers based on furnished information such as age, smoking habit status, alcohol consumption status, policy term and other parameters. Insurance company has deployed this business logic in the form of solidity contract on ethereum blockchain and has been using it successfully since years.

Since few months, few federal tax policies are changed by government and due to that insurance company's management decides to increase variable amount from $0 to $10 in business logic used to calculate premium amount.

They requested their blockchain team to change this business logic in already deployed contract but they received a shock of their life when they got to know from blockchain team that it's not possible to upgrade already deployed contracts on ethereum due to inherent immutability feature.

Management team then requested blockchain development team to implement right set of patterns to make all of their already deployed contracts to upgrade as needed. After few days, research development team came up with one solution. They implemented proxy contract pattern to achieve contract upgradation on ethereum network. They also explained the implementation techniques and challenges to management; which are mentioned in later in this section for everyone's benefit.

Let's try to implement the proxy-contract-architecture in this section similar to the one insurance company blockchain developers achieved. To accomplish this, let's create following six contract files:

"ProxyContractManager.sol" – This contract recipe is parent of proxyContract and UpgradeableContract. It manages methods, states, events for upgradable contracts.

```solidity
pragma solidity ^0.5.1;
//This contract is parent of proxyContract and UpgradeableContract. It
manages methods, states, events for upgradable contracts
contract ProxyContractManager {
  address public destinationAddr;
    event EventaddrUpgrade(address indexed newdestinationAddr, address
indexed olddestinationAddr, address sender);
    function delegateTo(address _destinationAddr) public;
}
```

"ProxyRegistry.sol" – This contract recipe is responsible to delegate calls to a destination (target) contract with delegate-call.

```solidity
//This contract is responsible to delegate calls to a target contract with
delegate-call opcode.
pragma solidity ^0.5.1;

import './ProxyContractManager.sol';
```

```
import './UpgradeableContract.sol';

contract ProxyRegistry is ProxyContractManager {
  //Firstly instantiate Proxy contract with first destination contract address
and emit event.
  constructor(address _destinationAddr) public {
    delegateTo(_destinationAddr);
  }


  //Delegate contract to a different destination contract.
  function delegateTo(address _destinationAddr) public {
    assert(destinationAddr != _destinationAddr);
    address olddestinationAddr = _destinationAddr;
    destinationAddr = _destinationAddr;
    emit EventaddrUpgrade(_destinationAddr, olddestinationAddr, msg.
sender);
  }


  //Fallback function that uses the delegatecall opcode to call business logic
from contract and retain proxy contract states.
  function () payable external {
    bytes memory msgData = msg.data;
    address target = destinationAddr;
    assembly {
      let ptr := mload(0x40)
      let size := returndatasize
      returndatacopy(ptr, 0, size)
            let result:= delegatecall(gas, target, add(msgData, 0x20),
mload(msgData), 0, 0)
      switch result
      case 0 { revert(ptr, size) }
      default { return(ptr, size) }
    }
  }
}
```

"ProxyContractManager.sol" – This contract recipe needs to be imported by any upgradeable contract to use ProxyRegistry contract methods.

```solidity
//Any upgradeable contract will import this contract to use proxy contract
delegateTo method.
pragma solidity ^0.5.1;
import './ProxyContractManager.sol';
contract UpgradeableContract is ProxyContractManager {
  function delegateTo(address) public {
    assert(false);
  }
}
```

"InsurancePremium.sol" – This contract recipe contains business logic for insurance company to calculate insurance premium based on user information such as age, alcohol consumption status, smoking habit affirmation and policy term.

```solidity
//Business logic contract for insurance company to calculate insurance
premium.
pragma solidity ^0.5.1;
import './UpgradeableContract.sol';
//Calculate insurance premium amount
//Use test data ("20", true, true, "9")
contract InsurancePremium {
  function Calculator(int age,bool is_smoke, bool is_consume_alcohol,int
time_period) public pure returns (int) {
    int variable_amount = 0;
    if(is_consume_alcohol){
      variable_amount = variable_amount + 100;
    }
    if(is_smoke){
      variable_amount = variable_amount + 100;
    }
```

```
        return ((variable_amount + (age + 50)) - time_period); //Random
logic to calculate insurance premium based on age, time duration, alcohol
consumption status and smoking habit affirmation
    }

}
```

"InsurancePremiumV1.sol" – This contract recipe contains changed (upgraded) business logic for insurance company to calculate insurance premium based on user information like age, alcohol consumption status, smoking habit affirmation and policy term. Insurance company has increased variable amount from 0 to 10 due to regulatory changes.

```
//Changed Business logic contract for insurance company to calculate
insurance premium.
pragma solidity ^0.5.1;
import './UpgradeableContract.sol';
//Calculate insurance premium amount
//Use test data ("20",true,true,"9")
contract InsurancePremiumV1 {
    function Calculator(int age,bool is_smoke, bool is_consume_alcohol,int
time_period) public pure returns (int) {
        int variable_amount = 10;
        if(is_consume_alcohol){
            variable_amount = variable_amount + 100;
        }
        if(is_smoke){
            variable_amount = variable_amount + 100;
        }
        return ((variable_amount + (age + 50)) - time_period);
//Random logic to calculate insurance amount based on age, time period,
alcohol consumption status and smoking habit affirmation
    }
}
```

"ProxyTest.sol" – This contract has been created to demonstrate how insurance company can trigger business logic call through ProxyRegistry contract and how ProxyRegistry contract fulfills request from upgraded contract (InsurancePremiumV1.sol) instead of old contract (InsurancePremium.sol).

```solidity
pragma solidity ^0.5.1;

import './ProxyRegistry.sol';
import './InsurancePremium.sol';
import './InsurancePremiumV1.sol';

/*This contract demonstrates the delegation of business logic from
ProxyRegistry contract. Proxy registry will execute insurance
business logic from the contract whose address is stored in destinationAddr
field.

*/
contract ProxyTest {
    ProxyRegistry pr;
    InsurancePremium ip;
    constructor(address payable _pr) public {
        pr = ProxyRegistry(_pr);
    }
    //Calculate insurance premium amount
    ("20",true,true,"9")

    function getInsurancePremium(int age,bool is_smoke, bool is_consume_
    alcohol,int time_period) public payable returns(int){
        ip = InsurancePremium(pr.destinationAddr()); //Business logic will
        depend on current destinationAddr that ProxyRegistry contract contains.
        return ip.Calculator(age,is_smoke, is_consume_alcohol,time_period);
        //Access public variable.
    }
}
```

Run on Remix Online Editor

We created six different contract recipes to achieve proxy pattern in solidity. Please follow instructions furnished below.

1. Open https://remix.ethereum.org. Create following six files on Remix.

   ProxyContractManager.sol –

```solidity
pragma solidity ^0.5.1;
//This contract is parent of proxyContract and UpgradeableContract. It
manages methods, states, events for upgradable contracts
contract ProxyContractManager {
  address public destinationAddr;
  event EventaddrUpgrade(address indexed newdestinationAddr, address
indexed olddestinationAddr, address sender);
  function delegateTo(address _destinationAddr) public;
}
```

   ProxyRegistry.sol –

```solidity
//This contract is responsible to delegate calls to a target contract with
delegate-call opcode.
pragma solidity ^0.5.1;

import './ProxyContractManager.sol';
import './UpgradeableContract.sol';
```

```solidity
contract ProxyRegistry is ProxyContractManager {
  //First of all instantiate Proxy contract with first destination contract
  address and emit event.
  constructor(address _destinationAddr) public {
    delegateTo(_destinationAddr);
  }


  //Delegate the contract to a different destination contract.
  function delegateTo(address _destinationAddr) public {
    assert(destinationAddr != _destinationAddr);
    address olddestinationAddr = _destinationAddr;
    destinationAddr = _destinationAddr;
      emit EventaddrUpgrade(_destinationAddr, olddestinationAddr, msg.
sender);
  }


  //Fallback function that uses the delegatecall opcode to call buisness logic
  from business logic contract and retains proxyRegistry contract states.
  function () payable external {
    bytes memory msgData = msg.data;
    address target = destinationAddr;
    assembly {
      let ptr := mload(0x40)
      let size := returndatasize
      returndatacopy(ptr, 0, size)
          let result := delegatecall(gas, target, add(msgData, 0x20),
mload(msgData), 0, 0)
      switch result
      case 0 { revert(ptr, size) }
      default { return(ptr, size) }
    }
  }
}
```

UpgradeableContract.sol –

```solidity
//Any upgradeable contract will import this contract to use proxy contract
delegateTo method.
pragma solidity ^0.5.1;
import './ProxyContractManager.sol';
contract UpgradeableContract is ProxyContractManager {
    function delegateTo(address) public {
        assert(false);
    }
}
```

InsurancePremium.sol –

```solidity
//Business logic contract for insurance company to calculate insurance
premium.
pragma solidity ^0.5.1;
import './UpgradeableContract.sol';
//Calculate insurance premium amount. Use test data - ("20",true,true,"9")
contract InsurancePremium {
    function Calculator(int age,bool is_smoke, bool is_consume_alcohol,int
time_period) public pure returns (int) {
        int variable_amount = 0;
        if(is_consume_alcohol){
            variable_amount = variable_amount + 100;
        }
        if(is_smoke){
            variable_amount = variable_amount + 100;
        }
```

```
        return ((variable_amount + (age + 50)) - time_period); //Random
logic to calculate insurance premium based on age, time duration, alcohol
consumption status and smoking habit affirmation
    }

}
```

InsurancePremiumV1.sol –

```
//Changed Business logic contract for insurance company to calculate
insurance premium.
pragma solidity ^0.5.1;
import './UpgradeableContract.sol';
//Calculate insurance premium amount. Use test data - ("20",true,true,"9")
contract InsurancePremiumV1 {
    function Calculator(int age,bool is_smoke, bool is_consume_alcohol,int
time_period) public pure returns (int) {
        int variable_amount = 10;
        if(is_consume_alcohol){
            variable_amount = variable_amount + 100;
        }
        if(is_smoke){
            variable_amount = variable_amount + 100;
        }
        return ((variable_amount + (age + 50)) - time_period); //Random
logic to calculate insurance premium based on age, time duration, alcohol
consumption status and smoking habit affirmation
    }

}
```

ProxyTest.sol –

```solidity
pragma solidity ^0.5.1;

import './ProxyRegistry.sol';
import './InsurancePremium.sol';
import './InsurancePremiumV1.sol';

/*This contract demonstrates the deligatiion of business logic from
ProxyRegistry contract. Proxy registry will execute insurance
businesslogic from the contract whose address is stored in destinationAddr
field.

*/
contract ProxyTest {
    ProxyRegistry pr;
    InsurancePremium ip;
    constructor(address payable _pr) public {
        pr = ProxyRegistry(_pr);
    }

    //Calculate insurance premium amount. Use test data - ("20",true,true,"9")
    function getInsurancePremium(int age,bool is_smoke, bool is_consume_
alcohol,int time_period) public payable returns(int){
        ip = InsurancePremium(pr.destinationAddr()); //Business logic will
depend on current destinationAddr that ProxyRegistry contract have.
        return ip.Calculator(age,is_smoke, is_consume_alcohol,time_period);
    }
}
```

2. Go to 'Run' tab on top right section.

3. Inside 'Run' choose environment in the dropdown to 'JavaScript VM'.

4. Sequence of contract code is of utmost importance hence please follow all the steps judiciously.

5. First deploy "InsurancePremium.sol" and copy deployed address of this contract.

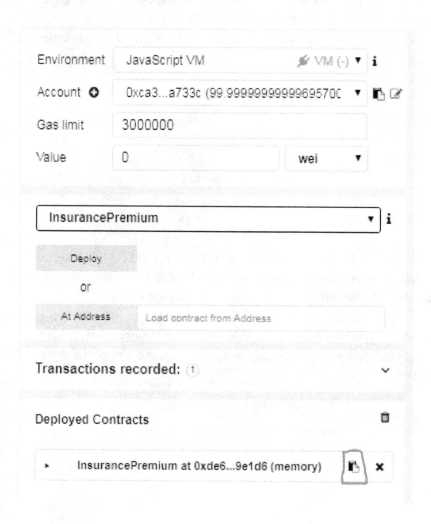

6. Deploy "ProxyRegistry.sol" contract with address copied from last step.

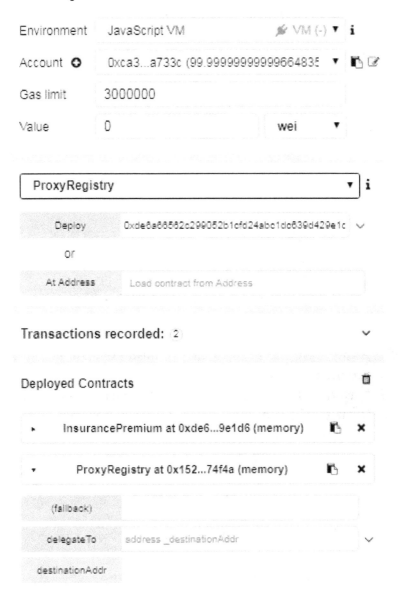

7. Use calculate method of contract "InsurancePremium.sol" with test data ("20",true,true,"9"). Post execution, you will witness premium amount as "$261".

8. As we have the need to change business logic for insurance premium calculation hence we have created contract "InsurancePremiumV1.sol" with new business logic, deployed it on blockchain and copied deployed contract address for ready reference.

9. Now let's try and execute business logic to calculate insurance premium with newly deployed business logic. This time with same data input ("20", true, true, "9"), readers will get different output i.e "$271".

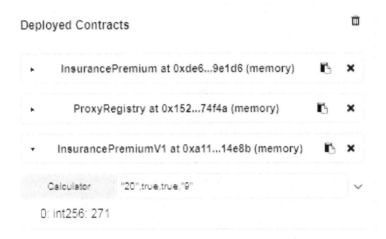

10. Now it is time to delegate business logic from "InsurancePremium. sol" to "InsurancePremiumV1.sol" using delegateTo() method of "ProxyRegistry.sol" Contract. Use delegateTo() method with copied address (deployed address of "InsurancePremiumV1.sol") from last step.

11. Congratulations! We have successfully upgraded our business logic to calculate insurance premium amount from contract "InsurancePremium.sol" to "InsurancePremiumV1.sol".

12. Now it is time to check whether insurance company premium calculation is updated with new business logic or not. To inference this, we need to deploy another contract "ProxyTest. sol" with deployed address of "ProxyRegistry.sol" and then execute its method "getInsurancePremium()" with same input ("20", true, true, "9"). You will get output as "$271". Hurrah!! Insurance company business logic has been updated and smart contract is able to refer new business logic. Congratulations once again!!

Basic idea and real essence is to use a proxy contract to execute business logic for insurance company instead of calling any business logic contract directly. Proxy contract will decide which business logic needs to be invoked.

Proxy contract "ProxyRegistry.sol" in this case uses "destinationAddr" field to save business-logic contract address. This provides "delegateTo()" function to set business-logic contract address. By using this method insurance company can adjust or delegate business-logic contract address as needed.

```
function delegateTo(address _destinationAddr) public {
    assert(destinationAddr != _destinationAddr);
    address olddestinationAddr = _destinationAddr;
    destinationAddr = _destinationAddr;
    emit EventaddrUpgrade(_destinationAddr, olddestinationAddr, msg.
sender);
}
```

We have furnished contract named "ProxyTest.sol" to demonstrate steps to call business-logic contract through proxy contract. Refer to code recipe below:

```
contract ProxyTest {
  ProxyRegistry pr;
  InsurancePremium ip;
  constructor(address payable _pr) public {
    pr = ProxyRegistry(_pr);
  }


  //Calculate insurance premium amount with test data
("20",true,true,"9")
  function getInsurancePremium(int age,bool is_smoke, bool is_consume_
alcohol,int time_period) public payable returns(int){
      ip = InsurancePremium(pr.destinationAddr()); //Business logic will
depend on current destinationAddr
      return ip.Calculator(age,is_smoke, is_consume_alcohol,time_period);
  }
}
```

The proxy contract also has one fallback function as depicted below. This is very important for readers to understand this aspect in right spirit to reap full potential.

```
//Fallback function that uses delegatecall opcode to call business logic from
business logic contract and retain proxyRegistry contract states.
  function () payable external {
    bytes memory msgData = msg.data;
    address target = destinationAddr;
    assembly {
      let ptr := mload(0x40)
      let size := returndatasize
      returndatacopy(ptr, 0, size)
          let result := delegatecall(gas, target, add(msgData, 0x20),
mload(msgData), 0, 0)
      switch result
      case 0 { revert(ptr, size) }
      default { return(ptr, size) }
    }
  }
}
```

Fallback function gets executed if remote contract or client attempts to execute any function; which proxy contract i.e. "proxyRegistry. sol" does not support. In that case, fallback function executes using delegatecall opcode to call right business-logic contract in proxy contract context (i.e. retain proxyRegistry contract states like msg. value and msg.sender).

Additional Context

Ethereum network scaling also has direct impact on solidity smart contract scaling. Although explaining network scaling strategies in detail is out of scope for this practical programming book however for reader's benefit, we will confer prominent strategies and terminologies concisely. Please refer these as follows:

Off-chain: Any transaction or activity not performed on a blockchain is off-chain operation. This refers to transactions not getting processed on the main chain.

Side-Chains: These are supplementary blockchains running in parallel to the main chain. Both main and supplementary chains interact based on business logic as needed.

Sharding: Sharding in the Blockchain world is similar to database sharding used in traditional and erstwhile solutions. In traditional databases, a shard is a horizontal partition of data in the database. Each shard is stored on a separate database server. This helps spread the load across servers. Likewise, in Blockchain world, Sharding has complete state of the Blockchain segregated into several shards. Overall state gets fragmented into smaller units and each unit will be stored by different nodes in the network. Transactions on the network are load balanced to different nodes depending on which shard they represent. Practically a shard only processes one fragment of overall state using parallel processing.

Lightning: Lightning Network is an off-chain scaling mechanism that enables transactions to get executed off-chain rather than on-chain. This is accomplished through channels. This enables users to execute transactions such as exchange of cryptocurrencies without making blockchain to validate transactions. Sole purpose of blockchain here is to create and close the payment channel, rest of the proceedings take place off-chain.

The Lightning network's aim is to make smart contract trading off the blockchain resulting in lower cost and supersonic speed of transactions. This is achieved by creating a channel that represents a smart contract. This enhances the speed of a transaction process as chunk of transactions are processed off the ledger.

The Lightning network has the potential to execute billions of transactions per second. Once achieved, this will be an unprecedented breakthrough in the blockchain world.

Raiden: Raiden is the implementation of Lightning on the Ethereum platform. Raiden Network claims to make Ethereum scalable to one million transactions per second. As more and more people trade with Raiden rather than on blockchain, transaction speed will increase and cost will come down. Raiden works with any ERC20-compliant token rather than just one currency such as Bitcoin's Lightning. Both systems are pushing for agreements that take load off the main ledger, which could improve the speed and overall cost of the cryptocurrency landscape. This will revolutionize the transaction rate.

Plasma: Plasma is a Blockchain scaling solution that uses child chains reporting to root chains to increase transaction rate without compromising the security concerns that usually are associated with smaller chains.

Here are Building Blocks of Plasma

Client—Watches Ethereum and runs the child chain, detecting fraudulent behavior as soon as possible and exiting as needed.

Child chain—Watches Ethereum for deposits and performs all computations regarding the current state of the chain.

Root chain—Anchors child chains to Ethereum via smart contracts. Handles deposits and exits for child chain, receiving only enough information to process both as well as to confirm or deny fraudulent exits.

Parent chain—Secures a child chain. Synonymous with Root chain for the Minimum Viable Product. In Plasma's final form there may be multiple parent chains between a child chain and a root chain.

To use a Plasma chain, users need to move their assets (i.e. Ether or tokens) from a parent chain to a child chain. To perform a deposit, users move assets from a parent chain to a child chain by transferring them to the appropriate Plasma smart contract on Ethereum. It is the Proof of Authority. If an invalid transaction is included in the child chain, everyone must exit the child chain immediately. The child chain relies on block confirmations. Result is huge improvement in scalability.

Solidity Programming Best Practices to Write Scalable Code

Introduction

Solidity provides many patterns to make code scalable and maintainable. Scalable code is a boon to developers to enhance existing code easily and upgrade when needed rather quickly. We already have seen Proxy upgradeability pattern in last section and in this section, we will elaborate on interface and library concepts to make solidity code scalable.

Pre Deep Dive Considerations

- Launch VS code editor to write and edit code.

- Create a new folder inside folder 'solidity_programming_practical_samples' and name it "Reviewing Scalability Principles" if you have not created yet.

- Open Remix online editor on browser to compile and run the recipe code.

- We have used "library_solution_uint.sol" contract example to demonstrate the working of library. Please open code in VScode

```solidity
pragma solidity ^0.5.1;
import "./SafeMath.sol";
contract secureIntegerFlow{
//Change name from Insecure to Secure as we have implemented SafeMath
solution.
    mapping (address => uint256) public balanceOf;


    // Vulnerable and insecure code
    function transfer(address _to, uint256 _value) public { //Try arguments
(0xca35b7d915458ef540ade6068dfe2f44e8fa733c,200) on remix.
        balanceOf[msg.sender] = 100; //Set balance of code executer address
to 100.
        /* Check if sender has balance
can cause integer overflow. balances[msg.sender] - _value >= 0 condition
is always satisfied because uint minus uint operation always results uint and
uint is always greater or equal to 0.


We have set sender address balance to 100. We require to check that
transfer occurs only when sender has sufficient balance to send money
i.e balanceOf[msg.sender] - _value >= 0. Due to interger overflow reasons
that we explained above condition balanceOf[msg.sender] - _value >= 0 is
always true. Thus sender can transfer any amount to destination address.*/
        require(balanceOf[msg.sender] - _value >= 0);
//This line of code can create disaster.
        require(SafeMath.sub(balanceOf[msg.sender],_value) >= 0);
//This line of code is now protected using SafeMath Lib.
        /* Add and subtract new balances */
        balanceOf[msg.sender] -= _value;
        balanceOf[_to] += _value;
    }
}
```

- We have used "interface.sol" contract example to demonstrate the working of interface. Please open code in VScode

```solidity
pragma solidity ^0.5.1;

/**
 * @title Insurance interface
 */
interface IInsurance {
    function approveInsurance() external returns (bool);
    function calculatePremium() external pure returns (string memory);
    function registerClaim() external returns (bool);
    function claimRelease() external returns (bool);
}
```

Code Recipes for Practical Learning

Library Approach: Library is commonly used code that any contract can use extensively. Library does not have any storage and even does not hold ether (payable and fallback functions are not available here). With help of libraries, we avoid repetitive code deployment on blockchain that saves gas (ether) needed for every repetitive code deployment.

Imagine an etherum world where every contract developer is leveraging already installed libraries and deploying their libraries to make usable for others. We will call it scalable ethereum world and we hope to see this turning into reality very soon.

Here is one example where we have used "SafeMath.sol" library to implement our contract logic.

```solidity
pragma solidity ^0.5.1;
import "./SafeMath.sol";
contract secureIntegerFlow{ //Change name from Insecure to Secure as we
have implemented SafeMath solution.
    mapping (address => uint256) public balanceOf;


    // Insecure Version
    function transfer(address _to, uint256 _value) public { //Try arguments
as (0xca35b7d915458ef540ade6068dfe2f44e8fa733c,200) on remix.
        balanceOf[msg.sender] = 100; //Set balance of code executer address
to 100.
```

/* Check if sender has balance as it can cause integer overflow. balances[msg.sender] – _value >= 0 condition is always satisfied because uint minus uint operation always results in uint. uint is always greater or equal to 0.

We have set sender address balance to 100. We need to check transfer occurs only when sender has sufficient balance to send money i.e. balanceOf[msg.sender] - _value >= 0. Due to integer overflow that we explained above, condition balanceOf[msg.sender] - _value >= 0 is always true. As a result sender can transfer any amount to destination address. */

```solidity
        require(balanceOf[msg.sender] - _value >= 0);
//This line of code can create havoc.
        require(SafeMath.sub(balanceOf[msg.sender],_value) >= 0);  //This
line of code is now protected using SafeMath Lib.
balanceOf[msg.sender] -= _value;
        balanceOf[_to] += _value;
    }
}
```

Interface Approach: By using "interface" we set a guiding contract so that no one can deploy any contract without implementing all the methods of interface or else EVM does not allow to deploy it. This makes developer's life easier and code scalable.

```
/**
 * @title Insurance interface
 */
interface IInsurance {
    function approveInsurance() external returns (bool);
    function calculatePremium() external pure returns (string memory);
    function registerClaim() external returns (bool);
    function claimRelease() external returns (bool);
}
```

Library Approach:

Library code deployed on ethereum address can be accessed by any contract using DELEGATECALL that ensures that library code gets executed in context of the calling contract. Library actually works as isolated piece of code that can only access state variables of calling contract if supplied explicitly. Library functions however can be called directly without using DELEGATECALL if those functions are "pure" or "view".

Interface Approach:

Interface allows other contracts to inherit it as parent contract. This ensures all contracts that implement it should behave uniformly i.e. child contracts must implement all methods available in interface else solidity will not allow its deployment.

On Remix, create following two files with furnished code recipe:

"test_interface.sol"

```
pragma solidity ^0.5.1;
import "./interface.sol";
/**
 * @title Insurance interface
 */
contract Insurance is IInsurance {
    function approveInsurance() external returns (bool){
        return true;
    }
}


"interface.sol".
pragma solidity ^0.5.1;

/**
 * @Title Insurance interface
 */
interface IInsurance {
    function approveInsurance() external returns (bool);
    function calculatePremium() external pure returns (string memory);
    function registerClaim() external returns (bool);
    function claimRelease() external returns (bool);
}
```

Now try to deploy "test_interface.sol" on remix. You will get error as depicted below:

This contract does not implement all functions and thus cannot be created.

OK

Hope this clarifies.

Additional Context

OpenZeppelin like open-source communities have many open source libraries that can be used by any developer. Interestingly they have used interface approach at several places to make their contracts scalable - https://openzeppelin.org/

Summary

In last few years, blockchain has attracted interest of lots and as a result transactions are growing rapidly. This has impacted blockchain size, network difficulty, transaction fee and turnaround time. This is high time that scaling drives wider acceptance of blockchain in critical areas of operation. This chapter was focussed on the scaling strategies to enhance the applicability of blockchain. Readers will benefit from the patterns explained and can use them in diverse areas. There are several solutions being researched around the globe and soon biggest challenge in blochain's wider acceptance will see concrete solution. Stay tuned !

CHAPTER 5

Implementing Security Techniques

Introduction

Solidity has very strong security principles however there have been instances where hackers have tapped the vulnerabilities and created havoc. From this chapter, readers will get a glimpse of prominent solidity code hacks, security strategies and architectural best practices that will be helpful in drafting a highly secure solidity programming solution that cannot be hacked.

Learning outcomes:

- Identifying and curbing reentrancy attack

- Identifying and restricting denial of services attack

- Identifying and curtailing integer overflow attack

- Comprehend security practices and strategies

Technical Requirements

Basic understanding of blockchain basics and ethereum:

- Readers should go through all other chapters of this book before reading this chapter.

- Readers should know about ethereum and ethereum virtual machine(EVM) - https://solidity.readthedocs.io/en/latest/introduction-to-smart-contracts.html#index-6

Setup coding environment:

- Install visual studio code for Windows/Linux/Mac from https://code.visualstudio.com/

- Install Solidity visual studio code extension from visual studio market place - https://marketplace.visualstudio.com/items?itemName=JuanBlanco.solidity

- Install extension for material icon theme

Pre Deep Dive Considerations

- Launch VS code editor to write and edit code.

- Create a new folder inside folder 'solidity_programming_practical_samples' and name it "Security Practices".

- Open Remix online editor on browser to compile and run the recipe code.

Identify and Curtail Reentrancy Attacks

Introduction

Solidity contracts have ability to call external contracts and send ether to external addresses. To attain this ability, solidity contracts generally make an external call to external contracts. External calls can be vulnerable if contract is not well fortified. Lack of protection can make contract hijacked by malicious users forcing the contract to execute recursive code through fallback function. This is known as reentrancy attack where attackers can re-enter contract code and control flow of execution OR can execute code at vulnerable spots of contract to create havoc.

Reentrancy vulnerabilities are mistakes that programmers commit in code to make their contracts victim for reentrancy attack.

Code Recipes for Practical Learning

Create following files in VScode:

"Locker. Sol" – This contract is an ether locker that provides functions to deposit and withdraw ethers. Users can keep ethers in locker through deposit and can withdraw same amount of ethers from locker anytime. We intentionally created this contract with code vulnerability so that attackers can leverage it to make reentrancy attack. We will discuss code vulnerabilities next.

```solidity
pragma solidity ^0.5.1;

//Locker contract allows deposit and withdrawal of ethers
contract Locker {
    mapping (address => uint) public userBalances; //Keep balance for addresses
    event Deposit(uint256 userBalance, address sender, uint amount);
    function deposit() public payable { //Unsafe deposit method
        userBalances[msg.sender] = msg.value;
        emit Deposit(userBalances[msg.sender], msg.sender, msg.value);
    }

    constructor() public payable { //Constructor method
    }

    function withdraw() public payable { //Unsafe withdrawal method
        uint256 amount = userBalances[msg.sender]; //Ascertain sender's balance
        //External function call to transfer ethers
        (bool success, ) = msg.sender.call.value(amount)(" ");
        if(!success) {
            //Handle failure code
        }
```

```
        userBalances[msg.sender] = 0;//After balance transfer, reset balance
to zero
    }

    function chkBalance() public view returns (uint256){ // Ascertain
balance for this contract
        return address(this).balance;
    }
}
```

"Reentrancy. Sol" – Attacker has created this contract to hijack external call of "Locker.sol" contract with reentrancy attack. With this contract, attacker will try to steal ethers from Locker contract account.

```
pragma solidity ^0.5.1;

import "./Locker.sol"; //Import victim "Locker" contract

contract Reentrancy {
    Locker public locker;
    constructor(address lockerAddress) public { /Constructor method
        locker = Locker(lockerAddress); //Instantiate the Locker contract
    }

    function deposit() external payable { //Deposit to Locker. Test data -
1000 Wei
        locker.deposit.value(msg.value)();
    }

    function hack_withdraw() external payable { //Withdrawal from Locker.
Test Data - 1000 Wei
        locker.withdraw();
    }
```

```
function chkBalance() public view returns (uint256){ //Balance of
current contract
    return address(this).balance;
}

function() external payable { // Fallback function
    if (address(locker).balance != 0 ) { //Hack if Locker contract has
balance else do not hack
    locker.withdraw(); //Re-enter the Locker
    }
  }
}
```

Run on Remix Online Editor

Reading comments inside code recipes is equally important thus please do not overlook them.

1. Open https://remix.ethereum.org. Create two files in "BROWSERS" section named "Locker.sol" and "Reentrancy. Sol". Paste corresponding code from your VScode in these files.

2. Go to 'RUN" tab on the right top panel.

3. Inside 'RUN" tab choose environment in the dropdown to 'JavaScript VM'. Remix provides many test accounts with balance of 100 ethers each. You can choose any default account from dropdown.

4. Deployment order of contracts is very important because in code we are using deploy address of "Locker.sol" in constructor while deploying "Reentrancy.sol". As a result, "Locker.sol" should be deployed first. We will be deploying "Locker. sol" contract with 10 ethers as its initial balance. Please see screenshot carefully to follow the deployment steps.

After deployment, copy address of deployed contract and deploy "Reentrancy.sol" with copied address. Refer screenshot below:

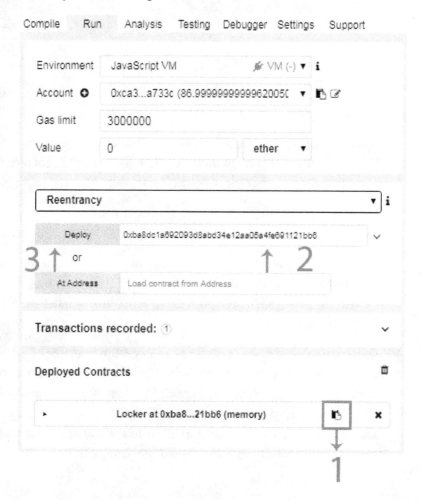

5. We have both contracts deployed now. Let's try Reentrancy attack on victim "Locker.sol" contract from "Reentrancy. sol" contract. Please follow steps basis furnished screenshot carefully to cheat "Locker.sol" contract account for ethers.

6. As described above, "Locker.sol" is a contract that allows users to deposit ethers with its "deposit ()" method and withdraw same amount of ethers with its "withdraw ()" method.

7. In this step, attacker "Reentrancy.sol" contract will deposit 50000 wei to Locker contract. See screenshot below.

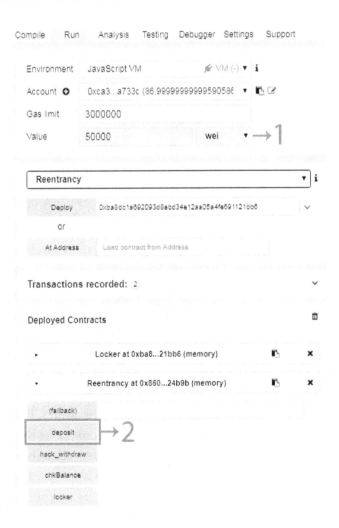

After this deposit, "Locker.sol" balance will increase from "10000000000000000000" to "10000000000000050000". Let's verify this with "chkBalance()" method. You will see output as given below:

8. After depositing "50000 wei" to locker, "Reentrancy.sol" contract will attempt a malicious hack with its "hack_ withdraw()" method. This method will send withdrawal request to "Locker.sol" contract when "Locker.sol" contract sends an external call to transfer funds to "Reentrancy.sol" contract. Attacker will hijack external call and execute "hack_ withdraw()" method again and again through its "fallback()" method. Re-entry attempt will continue until transaction gas gets consumed completely. After the attack if you verify account balance pertaining to both the contracts then you can easily understand that "Reentrancy.sol" has actually withdrawn "2950000" wei instead of "50000". This was a successful reentrancy attack ☹.

Curtail Reentrancy Attack

First and foremost, let's understand code vulnerability in "Locker.sol" that triggered the reentrancy. Let's focus on "withdraw ()" method inside "Locker.sol".

```
function withdraw() public payable { //Unsafe withdrawal method
        uint256 amount = userBalances[msg.sender]; //Ascertain sender's
balance
        //External function call to transfer ethers
        (bool success, ) = msg.sender.call.value(amount)(" ");
        if(!success) {
        //Handle vulnerable code
        }
        userBalances[msg.sender] = 0;
//After balance transfer, reset balance to zero
        }
```

This method used "call()" to transfer ethers to external contract address as depicted below:

```
(bool success, ) = msg.sender.call.value(amount)(" ");
```

External contract method i.e "fallback()" was invoked here to achieve fund transfer to external contract address.

By using "call()" method, "Locker.sol" contract enabled external contract to perform complex business logic in "fallback()" method as "call()" advances available gas (3000000 in our example. See remix screenshot above) to external contract as compared to "transfer()" and "send()" methods; which has stipulation of 2300 gas to external contract. This is only good enough to log an event in "fallback()" method.

Hackers/Attackers took advantage of "call()" method and wrote its "fallback()" method to re-enter "locker.sol" contract to execute "withdraw()" method many a times to steal ethers.

```
function() external payable { // Fallback function
        if (address(locker).balance != 0 ) { //Hack if Locker contract has
balance else do not hack.
        locker.withdraw(); //Re-enter Locker
    }
}
```

Let's now discuss good practices to curb reentrancy.

Any State Change Should Happen Before External Call

In "withdraw()" method, we are adjusting user balance after external function call; which is equal party in facilitating reentrancy attack. Adjusting user account balance is a state change for contract and it should never happen after any external call. To curtail reentrancy attack, let's alter "withdraw()" method and make state change adjustment before external call.

```
function withdraw() public payable { //Safe withdrawal method
        uint256 amount = userBalances[msg.sender]; //Ascertain sender's
balance

    userBalances[msg.sender] = 0;
//Before balance transfer, reset balance to zero
    //External function call to transfer ethers
    (bool success, ) = msg.sender.call.value(amount)(" ");
    if(!success) {
      //Handle failure code
    }
  }
```

With above changes in code, follow the steps all over again that we did perform in "Run on Remix Online Editor" section to deploy contracts. Thereafter run "Locker.sol" and "Reentrancy.sol". In last step when you will perform "hack_withdraw()", it will execute successfully and reentrancy will not hamper business logic anymore. See screenshot below:

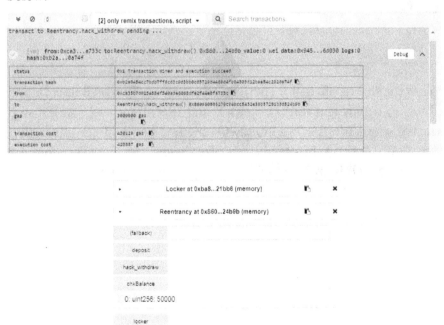

Use Transfer () and Send ():

Instead of using "call()", readers should use "transfer()" or "send()" as they allow only 2300 gas as stipend to external contract. As a result, external contract "fallback()" method cannot perform any complex logic inside it such as reentrancy attack. 2300 gas is only enough to log events in "fallback()" method.

"transfer()" is considered safer as it also throw exception (revert) when transaction fails while "call()" and "send()" only returns false.

Let's change "withdraw()" method inside "Locker.sol" contract and try to use "transfer()" instead of "call()".

```
function withdraw() public payable { //Safe withdrawal method
        uint256 amount = userBalances[msg.sender]; //Ascertain sender's
balance
        //External function call to transfer ethers
        msg.sender.transfer(amount);


userBalances[msg.sender] = 0;
//After balance transfer, reset balance to zero
    }
```

Follow the steps again that we performed in section "Run on Remix Online Editor" to deploy and run "Locker.sol" and "Reentrancy.sol". At last step when you execute "hack_withdraw()" method you will get transaction exception (Revert) in Remix log like below. So attacker contract "Reentrancy.sol" is unable to withdraw any amount if it try to hack.

Now, let's use "send()" in "withdraw()" method of "Locker.sol".

```
function withdraw() public payable { //Safe withdrawal method.
      uint256 amount = userBalances[msg.sender]; //Ascertain sender's
balance
      //External function call to transfer ethers
      msg.sender.send(amount);


userBalances[msg.sender] = 0;
//After balance transfer, reset balance to zero
    }
```

Follow the steps again that we performed in section "Run on Remix Online Editor" to deploy and run "Locker.sol" and "Reentrancy.sol". With "send()", last step where we call "hack_withdraw()" will not render any exception and transaction gets executed successfully as it does not throw exception as done by "transfer()". It will however not transfer any fund to attacker's contract "Reentrancy.sol". Check the final balance of "Reentrancy.sol" contract using "chkBalance()", it will output zero only.

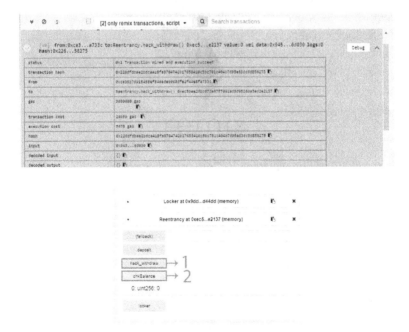

Disclaimer – Use of transfer() and send() is a good practice to protect against reentrancy but for the cases where we want to avoid contracts decelerating with gas cost changes, call() is a good choice.

Use Mutex to Lock States

In solidity, we use mutex to protect contracts against race conditions. This is very effective in curbing reentrancy as it locks states of contract before execution of any external call and unlocks it when execution ends. Let's use mutex in "Locker.sol" contract.

```
pragma solidity ^0.5.1;

//Locker contract allows deposit and withdrawal of ethers
contract Locker {
    mapping (address => uint) public userBalances; //Keep balance for addresses
    event Deposit(uint256 userBalance, address sender, uint amount);
    bool private Mutexlock;
    function deposit() public payable returns (bool) {
        /*Ascertain if Mutexlock is unlocked before proceeding further*/
        require(!Mutexlock);     /*lock, execute, unlock */
        Mutexlock = true;
        userBalances[msg.sender] = msg.value;
        emit Deposit(userBalances[msg.sender], msg.sender, msg.value);
        Mutexlock = false;
        return true;
    }

    constructor() public payable { //Constructor method
    }

    function withdraw() public payable returns(bool) {
```

```
        uint256 amount = userBalances[msg.sender]; //Ascertain sender's
balance
        require(!Mutexlock);      /*lock, execute, unlock*/
        Mutexlock = true;
        //External function call to transfer ethers
        (bool success, ) = msg.sender.call.value(amount)(" ");
        if(!success) {
          //Handle failure code
        }
        userBalances[msg.sender] = 0;
//After balance transfer, reset balance to zero
        Mutexlock = false;
        return true;
    }


    function chkBalance() public view returns (uint256){ //Ascertain balance
of this contract
        return address(this).balance;
    }
}
```

After introducing mutex in "Locker.sol", let's follow the steps all over again that we did perform in section "Run on Remix Online Editor" to deploy contracts. Thereafter run "Locker.sol" and "Reentrancy. sol". At last step where we call "hack_withdraw()", transaction will get executed successfully but no ether transfer to external attacker contract (Reentrancy.sol) will take place.

Note: Mutex is also very useful in preventing cross-function reentrancy attack and cross-function race conditions.

OpenZeppelin is providing open source "ReentrancyGuard.sol" contract, if you do not want to implement your own - https://github. com/OpenZeppelin/openzeppelin-contracts/blob/master/contracts/ utils/ReentrancyGuard.sol

Disclaimer – However, while using mutex in code we should be very conscious in ensuring that there should be no deadlock or livelock in code.

Additional Context

Mark Methods Untrusted

In real world scenarios, we cannot avoid call to external contracts from other contracts. To standardize the procedure, guideline should be established to mark (tag) methods "untrusted" that make external calls along with methods that call or share state with any "untrusted" methods. Here is an example to accomplish this:

```
function Untrusteddeposit() public payable { //Untrusted deposit method
    userBalances[msg.sender] = msg.value;
    emit Deposit(userBalances[msg.sender], msg.sender, msg.value);
}

constructor() public payable { //Constructor
}
```

```
function Untrustedwithdraw() public payable { //Untrusted withdrawal
method
        uint256 amount = userBalances[msg.sender]; //Ascertain sender's
balance
    //External function call to transfer ethers
    (bool success, ) = msg.sender.call.value(amount)(" ");
    if(!success) {
    //Handle failure code
    }
        userBalances[msg.sender] = 0;//After balance transfer, reset balance
to zero
    }
```

Identify and Curtail DOS Attacks

Pre Deep Dive Considerations

In denial of service attack, an external contract makes parent contract services inoperable temporarily or permanently. There are many ways an external contract can make another contract inoperable. We will discuss two prominent approaches in this section.

1. Unexpected Revert() through fallback () function

2. Block or consume entire gas Limit

Code Recipes for Practical Learning

External contract unexpected Revert () through fallback () function:

Create following files in VScode.

"myGame.sol" – This contract has some custom game rules. Some of the important rules are as follows:

- Any player can play this game

- We have created another contract "Player1" to play this game

- If player1 scores more than 100 then he will get a reward equal to the transaction value i.e "msg.value". If player1 scores less than 100 then there is no penalty levied on that player

- Contract "myGame" will transfer the reward amount to contract "player1" address each time when player1 scores more than 100

```solidity
pragma solidity ^0.5.1;
contract myGame {
   uint fixhighestScore = 100; //Highest score is 100 thus players have to
score above this stipulation to win


   constructor () public payable{} //Payable constructor


   function play(uint score, address payable contractAddr) external payable
{ //External play function
      if(score >= fixhighestScore){
         contractAddr.transfer(msg.value); // Transfer to Player1 contract
address. No one else can play if this external call fails
      }
   }


   function chkBalanceOfAccount() public view returns (uint256){ //Get
balance of account using which we execute contract on Remix
      return msg.sender.balance;
   }

   function () external payable{ //Payable fallback function


   }
}
```

"Player1.sol" – This is the external contract that a malicious player has created to perform DOS attack on "myGame.sol" contract.

```solidity
pragma solidity ^0.5.1;
import "./myGame.sol";
contract Player1{
    myGame mg;
    constructor (address payable _mg) public payable{ //Payable constructor
        mg = myGame(_mg); //Initialize myGame contract inside this contract
    }
    //Test data - (200)
    function playGame(uint score) public payable { //Call of function from myGame external contract
        mg.play.value(msg.value)(score,address(this));
    }


    function chkBalance() public view returns (uint256){ //Balance of palyer1 contract
        return address(this).balance;
    }


    function () external payable{ //Payable fallback function
        /*
        Case when external call fails due to malicious contract that throws error in fallback function. Due to this, every transfer to this contract will fail and cause ether loss in favour of account that triggered it.
        */
        revert();
    }
}
```

Run on Remix Online Editor:

To test it directly on remix, please follow below steps. Reading comments inside code recipes is equally important so please do not overlook them.

Open https://remix.ethereum.org. Create two files in "BROWSERS" section with name "myGame.sol" and "Player1.Sol". Paste the corresponding file code from your VScode to these file.

Go to "RUN" tab on right top panel.

1. Inside "RUN" tab, choose environment in the dropdown to 'JavaScript VM'. Remix will provide many test accounts with balance 100 ether each. You can choose default account from dropdown.

2. Deployment order is very important as in our code we are using deploy address of "myGame.sol" in constructor while deploying "Player1.sol".

3. Choose "myGame" contract from dropdown and deploy it. After successful deployment, copy deploy address of "myGame" contract.

4. Now choose "Player1" contract in the dropdown and deploy it with copied deploy address of "myGame".

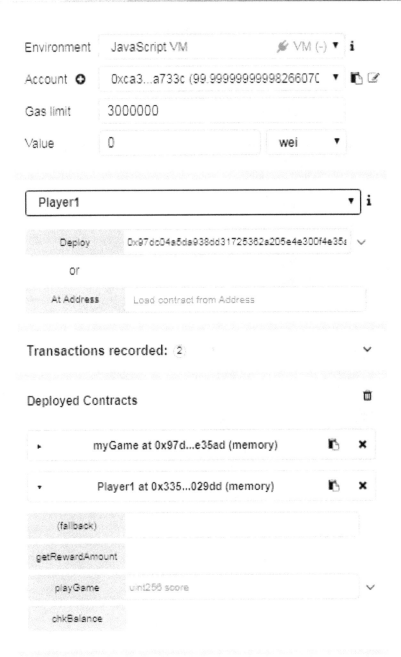

Environment   JavaScript VM   🔥 VM (-) ▼   i

Account ⊕   0xca3...a733c (99.99999999998266070   ▼   📋 ✎

Gas limit   3000000

Value   0   wei   ▼

Player1   ▼   i

Deploy   0x97dc04a5da938dd31725362a205e4e300f4e35a   ∨

or

At Address   Load contract from Address

Transactions recorded: 2   ∨

Deployed Contracts   🗑

▸   myGame at 0x97d...e35ad (memory)   📋   ✕

▾   Player1 at 0x335...029dd (memory)   📋   ✕

(fallback)

getRewardAmount

playGame   uint256 score   ∨

chkBalance

5. Thereafter let's try to execute "playGame()" method of "Player1.sol" contract.

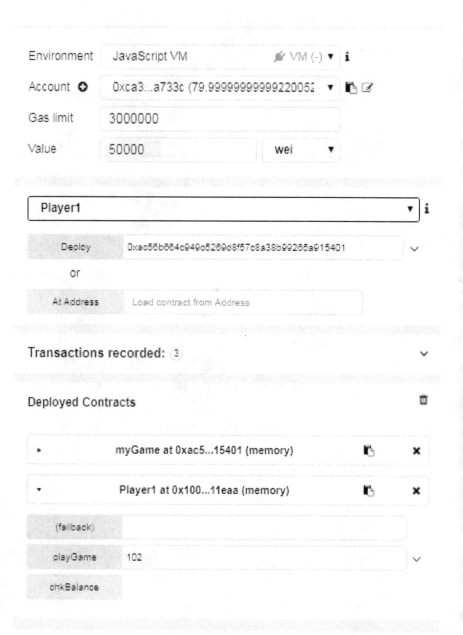

6. You will witness service denial in form of Revert opcode in Remix log.

```
transact to Player1.playGame pending ...

  [vn]  from:0xca3...a733c to:Player1.playGame(uint256) 0xf2b...80aef value:50000 wei data:0x587...000d9 logs:0    Debug  ∨
        hash:0x937...03e41

transact to Player1.playGame errored: VM error: revert.
revert  The transaction has been reverted to the initial state.
Note: The constructor should be payable if you send value.    Debug the transaction to get more information.
>
```

Block or Consume Gas Limit

In last DOS example, you did notice "revert()" opcode in "fallback()" function caused DOS. Good proposition however with "revert()" is that it returns remaining gas to main contract. In the same note, "assert()" opcode consumes all the dispatched gas from main contract. In this scenario, hackers using "assert()" to perform DOS on main contract by consuming all of its dispatched gas looks like below snippet:

```
function () payable {
    //Revert() returns the remaining gas but assert() consumes all the gas
    assert(1==2);
}
```

We can play around a bit by doing minor changes in "myGame.sol" and "Player1.sol" contracts.

```
pragma solidity ^0.5.1;
contract myGame {
    uint fixhighestScore = 100; //Highest score is 100. Players have to score
above this stipulation to win

    constructor () public payable{} //Payable constructor
```

```
    function play(uint score, address payable contractAddr) external payable
{ //External play function
    if(score >= fixhighestScore){
        (bool success, ) = contractAddr.call.value(msg.value)(" ");
        if(!success) {
        //Handle failure code
        }
    }
}


    function chkBalanceOfAccount() public view returns (uint256){ //Get
balance of account to execute contract on Remix
        return msg.sender.balance;
    }

    function () external payable{ //Payable fallback function

    }
}
```

In "myGame.sol", we did change "function play()" to use "call()" opcode instead of "transfer()". The reason as we know is "call()" dispatches all the gas to external contract but "transfer()" only dispatches 2300 gas as stipend. To see the impact of "assert()" in action, we need to make external call using "call()" opcode.

```
pragma solidity ^0.5.1;
import "./myGame.sol";

contract Player1{
    myGame mg;
    constructor (address payable _mg) public payable{ //Payable constructor
        mg = myGame(_mg); //Initialize myGame contract inside this contract
```

```
}

    function playGame(uint score) public payable { //Call of function from
myGame external contract
        mg.play.value(msg.value)(score,address(this));
    }


    function chkBalance() public view returns (uint256){ //Balance of
palyer1 contract
        return address(this).balance;
    }


    function () external payable {
        //Revert() returns the remaining gas but assert() consumes all the gas
        assert(1==2);
    }
}
```

In "Player1.sol", we have only changed "fallback()" function to use "assert()" as it consume all the gas.

Run on Remix Online Editor

You can run "myGame.sol" and "Player.sol" in same way as done before. In last step while executing "playGame()" method, you will observe that transaction was successful but did not update Player1 account. Reason - "assert()" consumed all the gas and caused DOS.

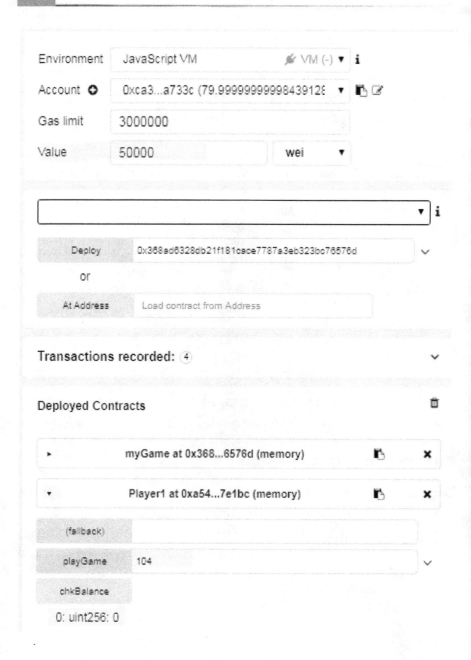

Gas consumption can be seen in Remix log as depicted below.

Curtail DOS Attack

Now, let's discuss some good practices to stop DOS. We need to follow all the good practices we learned in "Reentrancy" curtail section along with remedy measures mentioned below.

Prefer Pull Over Push for Fund Transfer

To resolve DOS, we need to do changes to allow pull reward over push reward in player's contracts.

We have implemented pull transfer in "myGame" in next code recipe. Instead of sending reward to players, we forced them to call "withdraw" function to pull reward. See below:

```
contract myGame {
----------------------

    function play(uint score, address payable contractAddr) external payable
    { //External play function
        if(score >= fixhighestScore){
            //Allow recipients to pull rewards using withdrawReward function
            rewards[contractAddr] = msg.value;
        }
    }
```

```solidity
    function withdrawReward(address payable _toReward) external payable
{ //Withdraw function
    uint reward = rewards[_toReward];
    rewards[_toReward] = 0;
    _toReward.transfer(reward);
    }


    -----------------------------

}

contract Player1{
    -----------------------------


    function getRewardAmount() public payable { //Pull reward amount
        mg.withdrawReward.value(msg.value)(address(this));
    }



    -----------------------------

}
```

Additional Context

Here are more best practices to prevent different type of attacks:

Handle unsigned Integer very carefully:

In solidity, if uint reaches its maximum value (2^{256}) then it will circle back to zero (overflow) and if uint goes below zero then it gets set to its maximum value (underflow). There are situations pertaining to integers that make them vulnerable.

Let's analyze an example below:

```solidity
pragma solidity ^0.5.1;
contract InsecureIntegerFlow{
    mapping (address => uint256) public balanceOf;
```

```
//Insecure and vulnerable code
function transfer(address _to, uint256 _value) public { //Try arguments
(0xca35b7d915458ef540ade6068dfe2f44e8fa733c,200) on remix.
    balanceOf[msg.sender] = 100; //Set balance of code executer address
to 100
    require(balanceOf[msg.sender] - _value >= 0); //This line can create
havoc
    /* Add and subtract new balance */
    balanceOf[msg.sender] -= _value;
    balanceOf[_to] += _value;
  }
}
```

Above code can create havoc as balances[msg.sender] – _value >= 0 condition is always satisfied since uint minus uint operation always produces uint and uint is always greater or equal to 0. With this proposition, it allows senders to transfer amount more than what they possess to other accounts that obscures contract state. Let's test it on remix.

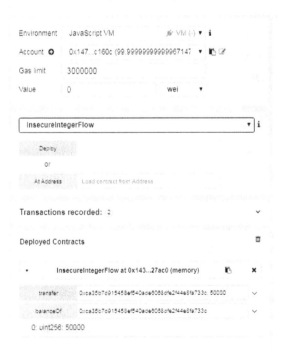

To handle this and other mathematical issues, we recommend to use SafeMath open source library from OpenZeppelin. You can find the library at https://github.com/OpenZeppelin/openzeppelin-contracts/blob/master/contracts/math/SafeMath.sol

In below example, we will use safeMath.sol to solve unsigned integer issues.

```
pragma solidity ^0.5.1;
import "./SafeMath.sol";
contract secureIntegerFlow{ //Change name from Insecure to Secure as we
have implemented SafeMath solution
    mapping (address => uint256) public balanceOf;
    // Secure Version
    function transfer(address _to, uint256 _value) public { //Try arguments
(0xca35b7d915458ef540ade6068dfe2f44e8fa733c,200) on remix.
        balanceOf[msg.sender] = 100; //Set balance of code executer address
to 100
        require(SafeMath.sub(balanceOf[msg.sender],_value) >= 0);  //This
line of code is now protected using SafeMath library
        /* Add and subtract new balances */
        balanceOf[msg.sender] -= _value;
        balanceOf[_to] += _value;
    }
}
```

Now, when you try to execute transfer() function with amount greater than 100 (actual balance of sender) then it should provide VM error like this in Remix console:

Use Invariants and Error While External Calls

While making external calls, we should protect our functions with invariants and with proper error handling. One of the example is below where we implemented a solution to curb reentrancy. Here we have used invariant "require" to protect function state.

In this example, we have also used error handling vis-à-vis external call.

```
(bool success, ) = msg.sender.call.value(amount)(" ");
    if(!success) {
      //Handle failure code
    }


function withdraw() public payable returns(bool) {
      uint256 amount = userBalances[msg.sender]; //Ascertain sender's
balance
      require(!Mutexlock);      /*lock, execute, unlock*/
      Mutexlock = true;
      //External function call to transfer ethers
      (bool success, ) = msg.sender.call.value(amount)(" ");
      if(!success) {
        // Handle failure code
      }
      userBalances[msg.sender] = 0;
//After balance transfer, reset balance to zero
      Mutexlock = false;
      return true;
    }
```

Summary:

Attackers always leverage the advantage of code vulnerabilities to perform security attacks. Solidity security best practices furnished in this chapter were designed based on known attacks thus far. When any new attack gets unveiled, this results in a new security practice or solution. Smart contract programmers always keep an eye on new vulnerabilities so that they can curtail them while writing code proactively. We strongly recommend you to become voracious readers and get yourself up-to-date to remain ahead of the curve. Wishing you wisdom in dealing with diverse situations.

CHAPTER 6

Using Truffle, Ganache, Geth & MetaMask

Introduction

In this chapter, we will elaborate steps to setup development environment using truffle, ganache, geth and metamask.

Truffle is primarily a development environment and testing framework for Ethereum blockchain.

Ganache-cli is a personal Ethereum Blockchain widely practiced to test smart contracts. Ganache is used to develop applications, deploy contracts, run tests and perform many other vital tasks privy to blockchain world.

Geth is the command line interface for running the full ethereum mining node.

Metamask enables users to run Ethereum DApps in the browsers without running full Ethereum node.

Learning outcomes:

- Set up Truffle the recommended way

- Link and initialize contracts

- Compile, deploy and run contracts

- Ganache and its Pseudo account generation

- Geth installation steps

- Ganache and Geth integration

- Metamask setup and readiness

Let's embark on the journey and learn the rules of the game.

Technical Requirements

Setup Coding Environment

- Install visual studio code for Windows/Linux/Mac from https://code.visualstudio.com/

- Install Solidity visual studio code extension from visual studio market place - **https://marketplace.visualstudio.com/ items?itemName=JuanBlanco.solidity**

- Install extension for material icon theme

Disclaimer – We are not promoting any tool or software. We have selected following tools and software based on our vast experience working on diverse blockchain projects.

Tool – Truffle Framework:

Requirements: NodeJS >= v8.9.4, Windows/Linux/Mac OS

Installation Steps:

- Open terminal or command prompt. You can also use VSCode terminal.

Run command "npm install -g truffle" on terminal. It will install seamlessly. On Windows, please follow specified pre-requisites and recommendation. Please refer official truffle site in-case you find any issue during installation: https://truffleframework.com/docs/truffle/ getting-started/installation

Tool - Installation of Ganache-cli:

Installation Steps:

- Open terminal or command prompt. You can also use VSCode terminal
- Run command "npm install -g ganache-cli" on terminal
- Read more about ganache on the official github link: https://github.com/trufflesuite/ganache-cli

Tool – Geth command line:

Installation procedure using brew is below:

brew update

brew upgrade

brew tap ethereum/ethereum

brew install ethereum

Installation of Geth in various ways can be accessed here:

https://github.com/ethereum/go-ethereum/wiki/Installing-Geth

Tool – Metamask

Chrome extension details can be referenced here:

https://chrome.google.com/webstore/detail/metamask/nkbihfbeogaeaoehlefnkodbefgpgknn

Setting up Truffle:

Introduction:

In this section, we are taking you through real time journey of setting up truffle project. We will init, compile our contracts in truffle project environment, and deploy those on ganache and geth using truffle commands.

Pre Deep Dive Considerations

- Launch VS code editor to write and edit code

- Create a new folder inside folder 'solidity_programming_practical_samples' and name it "Learn Tools"

- Launch truffle framework

- For demonstration purposes, we have emulated "single_inheritance.sol" from previous chapter. To demonstrate the deployment method of truffle and inheritance, we did fragment "single_inheritance.sol" file into two contract files namely

  1) "GeneralAgent.sol" and 2) "HealthInsuranceAgent.sol".

Code Recipes for Practical Learning

Disclaimer – In this book, we have used latest available version of Truffle v5.0.18 (core: 5.0.18) and Node v12.2.0. Truffle v5.0.18 has referred solc compiler version 0.5.0 that cannot compile code beyond 0.5.0. This is the reason of using pragma version '0.5.0' instead of '0.5.1' or beyond.

Create following files in VScode:

"HealthInsuranceAgent.sol"

```
pragma solidity ^0.5.1;
contract HealthInsuranceAgent {
  constructor() public {
    //No action for now
  }
  //Health insurance calculator
  int constant base_amount = 100;
    function insuranceAmountCalculator(int age,bool is_smoke, bool is_
consume_alcohol,int time_period) internal pure returns (int insurance_
amount) {
```

```
    int variable_amount = 0;
    if(is_consume_alcohol){
        variable_amount = variable_amount + 100;
    }
    if(is_smoke){
        variable_amount = variable_amount + 100;
    }
    return ((base_amount + variable_amount + (age + 50)) - time_period);
//Random logic to calculate insurance premium based on age, time duration,
alcohol consumption status and smoking habit affirmation
    }


    function checkEligibility(int age, int time_period) internal  pure returns
(bool is_insurance_possible) {
        //Random logic to ascertain insurance eligibility
        if (age > 60 || time_period > 40) { //Health insurance not allowed for
individuals with age > 60 years and term period > 40 years
            return false;
        }else{
            return true;
        }
    }
}
```

"GeneralAgent.sol" –

```
pragma solidity ^0.5.1;
import "./HealthInsuranceAgent.sol";
contract GeneralAgent is HealthInsuranceAgent {
    //Define mapping to store key-value pairs
    mapping(string => userRecord) userRecordMapping;

    //Organize user records using struct
```

```
struct userRecord
{
    string unique_identification;
    string name;
    int age;
    bool is_smoke;
    bool is_consume_alcohol;
    int time_period;
    bool has_health_insurance;
    int health_insurance_amount;
}
//Save user record. Test data to test on Remix -
("U123",20,"Jon",true,true,10,false,0)
function saveUserDetails(string memory unique_identification, int age,
string memory name, bool is_smoke, bool is_consume_alcohol, int time_
period, bool has_health_insurance, int health_insurance_amount) public
{
    userRecordMapping[unique_identification] = userRecord(unique_
identification, name, age, is_smoke, is_consume_alcohol, time_period,
has_health_insurance, health_insurance_amount);
}


//Responsible to offer health insurance. Test data to test on Remix -
("U123")
function doHealthInsurance(string memory unique_identification)
public payable returns (bool) {
    if(checkEligibility(userRecordMapping[unique_identification].age,
userRecordMapping[unique_identification].time_period)){ //Function
from parent contract
int insurance_amount =
insuranceAmountCalculator(userRecordMapping[unique_
identification].age,userRecordMapping[unique_identification].
is_smoke, userRecordMapping[unique_identification].is_consume_
alcohol,userRecordMapping[unique_identification].time_period);
        require(insurance_amount > 0); //Should be possitive number.
```

```
        userRecordMapping[unique_identification].health_insurance_
amount = insurance_amount;
        userRecordMapping[unique_identification].has_health_insurance
= true;
        return true;
    }else{
        return false;
    }
    }
    //Get user health insurance details - Test data to test on Remix -
("U123")
    function getUserDetails(string memory unique_identification) public
view returns(bool has_health_insurance, int health_insurance_amount){
        return (userRecordMapping[unique_identification].has_health_
insurance, userRecordMapping[unique_identification].health_insurance_
amount);
    }
}
```

Let us now setup our truffle project.

- Create a new folder "truffle-proj" under "solidity_programming_
  practical_samples/Tools".
  mkdir truffle-proj
  cd truffle-proj

- Initiate truffle project. This will create complete truffle project
  structure for you. You can find directories "contracts" and
  "migrations" in project structure.
  truffle init
  Above command will create following folders and files inside
  "truffle-proj" project:
  contracts/: Directory for solidity contracts
  migrations/: Directory for scriptable deployment files

test/: Directory for test files to test your application and contracts

truffle-config.js: Truffle configuration file

- Since we need to use ganache blockchain for development, let's setup "truffle-config.js" file real quick. On operating systems other than Windows, file name should be "truffle.js".

```
module.exports = {
 networks: {
  development: {
    host: "127.0.0.1",
    port: 8545,
    network_id: "*",
  },
 },
};
```

Linking, Initializing, Compiling Contracts

- Move contract files i.e "HealthInsuranceAgent.sol" and "GeneralAgent.sol" to "/contracts" folder under "truffle-proj" project.

- Now create a new file "2_deploy_contracts.js" within "/migrations" folder under "truffle-proj" project. Code inside this file allows us to deploy our contract files to ethereum blockchain network. Paste following code in this.

```
const GeneralAgent = artifacts.require("GeneralAgent");

module.exports = function(deployer) {
  deployer.deploy(GeneralAgent);
};
```

You probably would have noticed that we have stated only "General Agent" for deployment in "2_deploy_contracts.js" file specifically in the last step. The reason for this is inheritance property of solidity where parent (base) contract bytecode gets inline into child (derived) contract and finally a single contract is generated after deployment to EVM. We need to deploy only child contract i.e "General Agent" – Make a note of it.

- Now open terminal (VScode Terminal-1) and go to "truffle-proj" project directory. Now compile smart contracts using "truffle compile" command. You will get output as stated below.

  Compiling your contracts...
  ============================
  > Compiling.\contracts\GeneralAgent.sol
  > Compiling.\contracts\HealthInsuranceAgent.sol
  > Compiling.\contracts\Migrations.sol
  > Compiling.\contracts\HealthInsuranceAgent.sol
  > Artifacts written to D:\blockchain\Training\BTA Books\Book Chapters\Chapter6\Recipes\truffle-proj\build\contracts
  > Compiled successfully using:
  - solc: 0.5.0+commit.1d4f565a.Emscripten.clang

- Congratulations! We have successfully compiled contracts inside truffle project!!

Truffle employs "truffle compile" command to compile contracts. This command internally uses solc.js to compile solidity contracts.

Note: Truffle 5.0 and beyond, we can use our custom compiler too.

On first iteration, the tool will compile all the contracts; which are saved at "/contracts" directory. Subsequent iterations compile only updated or revised contracts since the last compilation.

After compilation, every contract gets saved inside "/build/ contracts/" directory in JSON format.

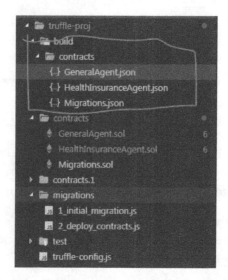

JSON format contracts inside "/build/contracts/" are considered artifacts. To get any artifact from truffle, we need to call it by corresponding artifact name. Here is an example that demonstrates it for "GeneralAgent" artifact.

```
const GeneralAgent = artifacts.require("GeneralAgent");
```

Additional Context

In truffle configuration file, we can override default directory path property for un-compiled contracts, compiled contracts, migration directories and many more.

```
module.exports = {
  contracts_directory: "./my_path_for_uncompiled_contracts",
  contracts_build_directory: "./my_path_for_compiled_contracts",
  migrations_directory: "./my_path_to_migration_directory",

  networks: {
    development: {
      host: "127.0.0.1",
```

```
    port: 8545,
    network_id: "*",
  }
 }
};
```

To know about other configurations, please refer: https://www.trufflesuite.com/docs/truffle/reference/configuration

Deployment on Ganache – Generation of Pseudo Accounts, Migration and Interaction with Contract

Introduction

In this section, we will explain prominent ways to deploy contracts to blockchain. We will also show-case hands on demonstration using ganache and geth tools.

Pre Deep Dive Considerations

- Launch VS code editor to write and edit code

- Create a new folder inside folder 'solidity_programming_practical_samples' and name it "Tools"

- Launch truffle framework.

- Open "truffle-proj" project that we created in the previous section

Code Recipes for Practical Learning

Now it's time to deploy our contracts to blockchain network. We can start our own ethereum blockchain using ganache-cli. Ganache comes under truffle suite. Read more about ganache on its official site - https://truffleframework.com/ganache

Open a new terminal (VScode Terminal-2) and go to "truffle-proj" project root directory. Execute command "ganache-cli". It will run ethereum blockchain with 10 default test accounts having 100 ethers each under their disposal. You will witness output as depicted below on your console:

```
Ganache CLI v6.4.3 (ganache-core: 2.5.5)

Available Accounts
==================
(0) 0x36c3a81f4ab49f6fb9afebf1c9431680266a6374 (~100 ETH)
(1) 0xfcaaecc84d1b9272ab1257712e1476c1767c4192 (~100 ETH)
(2) 0x06a6243b90773c48ec8c6d44053f0e3240a29c83 (~100 ETH)
(3) 0xb729d4b6613d95a601ac88718c75e55cbf6e97c9 (~100 ETH)
(4) 0x19b7b4c014726eaca976fbfcc3bc36b9b506ed79 (~100 ETH)
(5) 0x420ecf27c23cf004ebb04e7ac863a349f5a1d8c2 (~100 ETH)
(6) 0xc7941b4e65f8bfff41dbc9547a29757da25ff72e (~100 ETH)
(7) 0x15c58bb6fd3e1297ec8ef812f45047a55570fcb1 (~100 ETH)
(8) 0x31bb7074d0698e10cd4b1ea274e5533f29b2f44a (~100 ETH)
(9) 0x6c781bd7a72e2456e02ff8ad31839d640e384466 (~100 ETH)

Private Keys
==================
(0) 0x805511f9d61303d551432676305ac465e0d7d15d174779a299d0eb7ebb937a1c
(1) 0x04a2dc9ce9278becc350af0a6350c9eef2d45c56ba7bf793bde9fdd117da110b
(2) 0x49c72b5a05aad65d1b5e597c5ecf28308a6864e9aefa4cf2364fceb039a2aceb
(3) 0xf6dca3ba76561bcf5b33b2dc5a9257b6b44662eee945b894a6658019913364db
(4) 0xfb62a74766e08134c2e0f13bde07a542a35fe1bb6c19728a17398116bb2bac5e
(5) 0x43cd4353fc56b7f469625a8793b5eb6db17afcc12bfd5d725e725fa56d09effb
(6) 0x6ec309b32203a1c29eb49b4a1237b6383a2c1d3f678a20d003a30a101ba7df48
(7) 0xae792f8dfa7ef49012d1d6e7bc9656883bb8f8f386890cc1b12b38acc4e45605
(8) 0xefa478ff874527e0905e167e27bbccbe945cfc1091257db275e8c229ed525dc6
(9) 0xbca0f69dfb11745c1d857add7de44ee7d451497a280dd4f59d9abae980d8090a

HD Wallet
==================
Mnemonic:      bitter manage enroll canvas poem gorilla planet cheap medal enforce spend void
Base HD Path:  m/44'/60'/0'/0/{account_index}

Gas Price
==================
20000000000

Gas Limit
==================
6721975
```

We need to change configuration file of truffle-proj project i.e "tuffle-config.js" to instruct it to use ganache blockchain.

```
module.exports = {
 networks: {
  ganache: {
   host: "127.0.0.1",
```

```
port: 8545,
network_id: "*",
},
},
};
```

Now we need to open a new terminal (VScode Terminal-3) and execute command "truffle migrate --network ganache" from root of "truffle-proj". You will witness with a sigh of relief – Contract has deployed on ganache blockchain – Snapshot below for your reference:

```
2_deploy_contracts.js
=====================

  Deploying 'GeneralAgent'
  ------------------------
  > transaction hash:    0x6eee32ed3ada73f4ad46cae62dea685cf1d93986b606c492340f3578264ff321
  > Blocks: 0            Seconds: 0
  > contract address:    0x9e34F50D6d29F26346775F269DF1e4E013F26f2f
  > block number:        3
  > block timestamp:     1561319276
  > account:             0x36C3A81f4ab49F6fB9Afebf1C9431680266a6374
  > balance:             99.97712704
  > gas used:            816706
  > gas price:           20 gwei
  > value sent:          0 ETH
  > total cost:          0.01633412 ETH


  > Saving migration to chain.
  > Saving artifacts
  -------------------------------------
  > Total cost:          0.01633412 ETH
```

Congratulations! We have deployed all of our contracts successfully on ganache local blockchain.

Let's now interact with smart contracts. Open a new terminal (VScode Terminal-4) and then open truffle console using command "truffle console --network ganache". It will open ganache command line console as depicted below:

XXXX\truffle-proj>truffle console --network ganache

truffle(ganache)>

On truffle console, write following commands in the given sequence to:

- Create "GeneralAgent" contract instance

- Get account to execute contract

- Call method using contract instance

- truffle(ganache)> let instance = await GeneralAgent.deployed()

- undefined

- truffle(ganache)> let accounts = await web3.eth.getAccounts()

- undefined

- truffle(ganache)> instance.
  saveUserDetails("a001",24,"John",true,true, 20,false,100000,
  {from: accounts[0]})

You will see output of the last command as depicted below. Output itself demonstrates that there is no issue in executing "GeneralAgent" contract on blockchain. Congratulations!

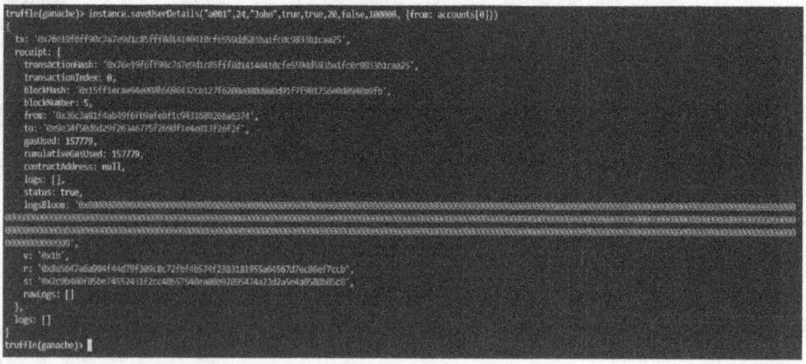

By default, ganache-cli runs on http://127.0.0.1:8545. As demonstrated above, to use ganache blockchain with truffle, below steps are vital:

- Truffle config file "truffle-config.js" has been forced to use ganache network

```
module.exports = {
 networks: {
  ganache: {
   host: "127.0.0.1",
   port: 8545,
   network_id: "*",
  },
 },
};
```

- We have forced migration of contracts on ganache network using command "truffle migrate --network ganache".

  Ganache in reality is a blockchain emulator; which allows us to execute and test solidity contracts without worrying too much about following challenges:

- Install and sync local blockchain node (Geth) on local machine [Not needed]

- Instant transaction mining [With no cost]

- Accounts reset, recycle and instantiation [Through ethers without mining]

We can use various options with Ganache-cli – Go through various options as follows:

https://docs.nethereum.com/en/latest/ethereum-and-clients/ganache-cli/

Additional Context

Ganache provides convenient desktop app (developed using electron technology) GUI. Here are the steps to install it on local machine.

- Open a new terminal on VScode (Terminal-5), create a folder named "ganache".

  mkdir ganache

- Clone ganache source code

cd ganache

git clone https://github.com/trufflesuite/ganache.git

- After source code download – Go to root of source code i.e "ganache" and install dependencies

  cd ganache
  npm install

- Run ganache using command "npm start" and click on "Quickstart" button at launch

- Once GUI is open, use "switch" button to switch networks

Private Blockchain Using Geth

Introduction

In this section, we will show-case optimum way to use geth to create accounts and run private blockchain on local machine. You will see use of Geth in depth while cooking a unique ethereum full-stack project recipe later in this book.

Pre Deep Dive Considerations

- Create a folder

- Launch VS code editor to write and edit code

- Open a new terminal on VScode (Terminal-6)

- As a pe-requisite, Geth should be installed on your system

Code Recipes for Practical Learning

Creating an Account Using Geth:

Use terminal-6 from any directory on your system and run command "geth account new". You need to enter passphrase to create account.

Note: You need to remember this passphrase as this needs to be passed in every transaction using Geth.

XXXX>geth account new

Your new account is locked with a password – Please create one. Keep this password handy.

Passphrase:

Repeat passphrase:

Address: {XXXXXXXXX}

"Address: { XXXXXXXXX }" is wallet address that gets saved on system with a private key in encrypted form. System locations can vary based on operating system you are using.

Mac OS: ~/Library/Ethereum

Linux OS: ~/.ethereum

Windows OS: %APPDATA%\Ethereum

Creating Geth Genesis Block

Genesis block is first block on blockchain. Geth provides "genesis.json" file to organize ethereum configuration and private blockchain state variables before launching blockchain. Most of the configurations are to be kept as default. Please replace "<My wallet address>" with your wallet address generated using "geth account new" command.

```
{
  "config": {
    "chainId": 0,
    "homesteadBlock": 0,
    "eip155Block": 0,
    "eip158Block": 0
  },
  "alloc": {
```

```
    "<My wallet address>": {
      "balance": "1000000000000000000000000000000000"
    }
  },
  "coinbase": "0x0000000000000000000000000000000000000000",
  "difficulty": "0x20000",
  "extraData": "",
  "gasLimit": "0x2fefd8",
  "nonce": "0x0000000000000042",
  "mixhash": "0x0000000000000000000000000000000000000000
000000000000000000",
  "parentHash": "0x0000000000000000000000000000000000000000
000000000000000000",
  "timestamp": "0x00"
}
```

Creating Private Blockchain Using Geth

Using Geth, you can run multi-node private blockchain on local machines. In this section - We will demonstrate steps to run a single node on local machine. We will scale this to multiple nodes later in this book. Run below commands in the given sequence:

- Create a new folder on your workstation named "PrivateNode1"

- Change directory to "PrivateNode1" using "cd PrivateNode1" command

- Copy "genesis.json" file to "PrivateNode1" folder

- Run command "geth --datadir. init genesis.json"

- You will witness output as depicted below:

```
D:\blockchain\Training\BTA Books\Book Chapters\Chapter6\PrivateNode1>geth --datadir . init genesis.json
WARN [06-24|23:48:39] No etherbase set and no accounts found as default
INFO [06-24|23:48:39] Allocated cache and file handles        database="D:\\blockchain\\Training\\BTA Books\\Book Chapters\\Chapter6\\PrivateNode1\\geth\\chaindata" cache=
16 handles=16
INFO [06-24|23:48:39] Writing custom genesis block
INFO [06-24|23:48:39] Successfully wrote genesis state        database=chaindata                                                                                      hash=5
e1fc7.d790e0
INFO [06-24|23:48:39] Allocated cache and file handles        database="D:\\blockchain\\Training\\BTA Books\\Book Chapters\\Chapter6\\PrivateNode1\\geth\\lightchaindata" c
ache=16 handles=16
INFO [06-24|23:48:39] Writing custom genesis block
INFO [06-24|23:48:39] Successfully wrote genesis state        database=lightchaindata                                                                                 h
ash=5e1fc7.d790e0

D:\blockchain\Training\BTA Books\Book Chapters\Chapter6\PrivateNode1>
```

- Above command will create following folder and file structure under the "PrivateNode1" directory

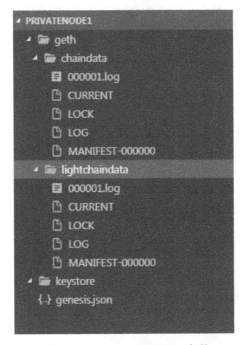

- Congratulations! You have successfully created a private ethereum node on your machine!

Interact with Private Node

Geth provides console to interact with running node. We can launch console using command "geth console" by providing anticipated node attributes as arguments. Commands for your ready reference are given as below:

- cd PrivateNode1

- geth --datadir. --networkid 0 --port 11111 --nodiscover console

- On console execute query "personal.listAccounts" to retrieve wallet address you configured in genesis.json file

- In above command "--datadir" is "PrivateNode1". "--networkid" is "chainId" that we had setup in genesis.json file

- "--nodiscover" indicates that we do not want to make node available to be discovered and connected by any other ethereum node running under the sun

- "--port" is port number where other nodes can connect to this peer node

To run a private ethereum network, we need to first create a genesis block (first block). This should contain all the essential information regarding network configuration along with details around peer connection with other private nodes in same network. We use "genesis.json" file to configure genesis block for private network. Let's understand each attribute in "genesis.json" file.

Config: As per ethereum source code (https://github.com/ethereum/go-ethereum/blob/feeccdf4ec1084b38dac112ff4f86809efd7c0e5/params/config.go#L71 struct datastructure contains all network related configurations.

```
type ChainConfig struct {
ChainId *big.Int `json:"chainId"` // Chain id identifies the current chain
and is used for replay protection
HomesteadBlock *big.Int `json:"homesteadBlock,omitempty"`
// Homestead switch block (nil = no fork, 0 = already homestead)
DAOForkBlock *big.Int `json:"daoForkBlock,omitempty"`
// TheDAO hard-fork switch block (nil = no fork)
DAOForkSupport bool `json:"daoForkSupport,omitempty"`
// Node supports or opposes DAO hard-fork
```

```
// EIP150 implements Gas price changes (https://github.com/ethereum/
EIPs/issues/150)
EIP150Block *big.Int `json:"eip150Block,omitempty"` // EIP150 HF block
(nil = no fork)
EIP150Hash common.Hash `json:"eip150Hash,omitempty"`
// EIP150 HF hash (fast sync aid)
EIP155Block *big.Int `json:"eip155Block,omitempty"`
// EIP155 HF block
EIP158Block *big.Int `json:"eip158Block,omitempty"`
// EIP158 HF block

// Various consensus engines
Ethash *EthashConfig `json:"ethash,omitempty"`
Clique *CliqueConfig `json:"clique,omitempty"`
}
```

chainID – This is identification Id for blockchain. Example - For mainnet, chainId is 1. This protects network from replay attack (https://en.wikipedia.org/wiki/Replay_attack). Ethereum uses this ID to distinguish transaction-signing methods.

HomesteadBlock – Inference from 0 refers to second major release of ethereum i.e. homestead to build network

DAOForkBlock – The block number (1920000th) where DOA attack took place in 2016. We have not used this in our "genesis.json" file.

Other parameters are related to EIP. This is abbreviation of "Ethereum Improvement Proposal" (https://github.com/ethereum/EIPs) and contains features that community has proposed for change or upgrade in Ethereum code or its approach primarily. Proposals may gets accepted and rejected after deliberations.

Including EIP, blocks in "genesis.json" file create blockchain. We recommend to use all EIPs if we are creating private network for enterprise use.

EIP150Block – It was accepted at block 2463000. Its implementation surged gas price as a result of response to denial-of-service attack.

EIP155Block – Related to relay attack prevention

EIP158Block – Related to empty account dealing of ethereum client

Additional Context

Connect Geth to Mainnet and Testnet

We can connect Geth client directly to Ethereum mainnet and testnet. Here is the command to accomplish this:

geth — testnet — data-dir="C:\EthereumTestnet" — rpc — rpcapi eth,web3,net,personal

geth — mainnet — data-dir="C:\EthereumMainnet" — rpc — rpcapi eth,web3,net,personal

Disclaimer – Mainnet data sync needs more than 100GB of system space while Testnet data needs more than 30 GB. Be cognizant of this before running above commands. ☺

Connect Geth to Ganache

This is not a common scenario where Geth needs to be integrated with locally running ganache. We do not recommend this either as it can potentially collapse or flunk due to blockchain incompatibility. Nevertheless, in case you need this in any peculiar situation then use following command.

geth attach http://127.0.0.1:8545

Interacting with the browser using Metamask Introduction

MetaMask allows users to run Ethereum DApps in leading browsers without running full Ethereum node. Readers can install MetaMask add-on in Chrome, Firefox, Opera and Brave browsers.

Pre Deep Dive Considerations

Open metamask guide in browser - https://metamask.io.

Code Recipes for Practical Learning

1. Click on *"Get Chrome Extension"* link.

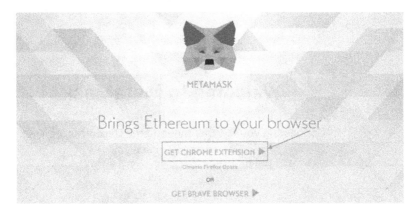

2. Click on *"Add to Chrome"* button on the opened tab:

3. Click on the *"Add Extension"* button.

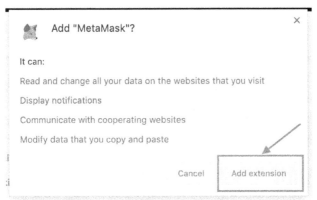

4. The extension has now been successfully installed/added to chrome. Click on *"Get Started"* to configure the account:

Welcome to MetaMask

Connecting you to Ethereum and the Decentralized Web.
We're happy to see you.

5. Click on *"Create a Wallet"* button to configure a new wallet.

 METAMASK

New to MetaMask?

6. Enter a new password and click on *"Create"* button.

 METAMASK

< Back

Create Password

New Password (min 8 chars)

```
••••••••••••
```

Confirm Password

```
••••••••••••
```

✔ I have read and agree to the Terms of Use

Create

7. Click on the box to reveal the secret words.

 METAMASK

Secret Backup Phrase

Your secret backup phrase makes it easy to back up
and restore your account.

WARNING: Never disclose your backup phrase. Anyone
with this phrase can take your Ether forever.

🔒

CLICK HERE TO REVEAL SECRET WORDS

Tips:

Store this phrase in a password
manager like 1Password.

Write this phrase on a piece of paper
and store in a secure location. If you
want even more security, write it
down on multiple pieces of paper
and store each in 2 - 3 different
locations.

Memorize this phrase.

Download this Secret Backup
Phrase and keep it stored safely on
an external encrypted hard drive or
storage medium.

8. Click on "*Next*" to move to the next step.

Secret Backup Phrase

Your secret backup phrase makes it easy to back up and restore your account.

WARNING: Never disclose your backup phrase. Anyone with this phrase can take your Ether forever.

> point butter hill unknown ritual sock sing victory estate whip surprise museum

Tips:

Store this phrase in a password manager like 1Password.

Write this phrase on a piece of paper and store in a secure location. If you want even more security, write it down on multiple pieces of paper and store each in 2 - 3 different locations.

Memorize this phrase.

Download this Secret Backup Phrase and keep it stored safely on an external encrypted hard drive or storage medium.

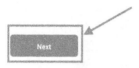

9. Confirm the Secret Backup Phrase by sequentially clicking on the respective words. Click on "*Confirm*".

< Back

Confirm your Secret Backup Phrase

Please select each phrase in order to make sure it is correct.

10. It is really important to keep the backup phrase safe. This will help in the recovery of wallet in future. Click on *"All Done"* button.

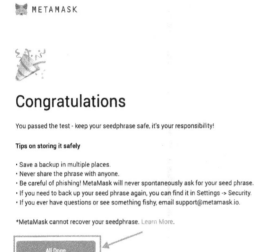

Congratulation!.Your metamask wallet has now been created successfully.

Code Recipes for Practical Learning

To purchase ethers and link to the wallet:

1. You can now click on the metamask icon in the chrome's plugins section to use it further.

2. Click on the Menu icon on the left top and then click on "Details".

3. You can here see the wallet details such as Barcode and Wallet address.

4. You can also copy wallet's address on the clipboard by directly clicking on the following.

5. Click on "Send" button to transfer tokens to other addresses.

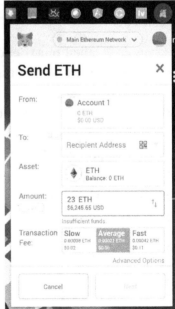

6. Some advanced options to send ethers are depicted here.

Summary

This chapter enabled our friends to install and get familiar with most prominent tools prevalent in the world of smart contracts as on today. We recommend readers to get familiar with installations using wide and diverse environments as real time projects will require you to be well versed with many more environment configurations and ecosystems. The more you practice, the more armors you attain that make you an expert in diverse practical circumstances. Do your hands dirty and be ready with all the answers. Good luck!

CHAPTER 7

Troubleshooting and Debugging

Introduction

Troubleshoot and debug words are used interchangeably in programming world though in real essence, they are slightly different. Troubleshoot is more leaned towards setting up an environment with right workflow encompassing pertinent protocols, tools and techniques to make system robust enough to detect issues on its own. Troubleshoot can also undertake issue fixes if they are related to environment.

Ethereum frameworks such as Truffle and IDEs like Remix are providing their own environment to troubleshoot diverse problems. They have established tools and techniques that developers can use to identify issues and then use programming techniques or pertinent tools to debug those issues in order to fix them.

In this chapter, we will see how we can troubleshoot and debug issues using Truffle framework. If you are using any framework other than Truffle for development, then go through corresponding official documents to get familiar with their troubleshooting and debugging methodology.

Additionally, we will see error and exceptional handling in real action. Using right error and exceptional handling, we can minimize many issues and corresponding debug opportunities.

Learning outcomes:

- Understanding the process to debug compile time errors.

- Understanding the mechanism to debug runtime errors.

- Understanding the process to debug logical errors.

- Understanding the mechanism to debug errors on Remix online IDE.

- Understand error and exception handling in Solidity code with practical examples and recipes.

- Understand the difference among Require(), Assert() and Revert() through practical code examples and recipes.

Technical Requirements

Basic Understanding of Blockchain Basics and Ethereum

- Readers should know and understand basics of blockchain - **https://solidity.readthedocs.io/en/latest/introduction-to-smart-contracts.html#blockchain-basics**

- Readers should know about ethereum and ethereum virtual machine(EVM) - https://solidity.readthedocs.io/en/latest/introduction-to-smart-contracts.html#index-6

Setup Coding Environment

- Install visual studio for Windows/Linux/Mac from **https://code.visualstudio.com/**

- Install Solidity visual studio code extension from visual studio market place - **https://marketplace.visualstudio.com/items?itemName=JuanBlanco.solidity**

- Install extension for material icon theme.

Installations

Disclaimer – We are not advertising or promoting any tool or software. We have chosen following tools and software based on our vast experience encompassing several blockchain projects.

Tool - Truffle Framework

Requirements: NodeJS >= v8.9.4, Windows/Linux/Mac OS

Installation Steps:

- Open terminal or command prompt. You can also use VSCode terminal.

Run command "npm install -g truffle" on terminal. It will install truffle for you. On Windows, please follow pre-requisites and recommendations. Please go to official truffle site in case you encounter any issues during installation - https://truffleframework.com/docs/truffle/getting-started/installation

Tool - Installation of Ganache-cli

Installation Steps:

- Open terminal or command prompt. You can also use VSCode terminal.

- Run command "npm install -g ganache-cli" on terminal.

Read more about ganache on its official github link - https://github.com/trufflesuite/ganache-cli

Troubleshooting and Debugging Approach and Best practices

Introduction

Usually troubleshooting process is of utmost importance with respect to issues detected by QA experts or end users. These errors are usually logical errors OR runtime errors however sometimes complex compile time errors also require solid debugging approach.

In this section, we will take you to the world of real time journey of troubleshooting, debugging and rectifying the contracts using truffle framework. To provide in-depth clarity, we will use three smart contracts that will produce compilation, logical and runtime errors respectively.

Compile Time Error – When error occurs at the time of compilation.

Runtime Error – When ethereum EVM finds issues in running the code.

Logical Error – When EVM detects no issues however code crashes due to program logic solely.

Pre Deep Dive Considerations

- Launch VS code editor to write and edit code.

- Create a new folder inside folder 'solidity_programming_practical_samples' and name it "Troubleshooting and Debugging".

- Open Remix online editor on browser to compile and run recipe code.

- Launch truffle framework.

Code Recipes for Practical Learning

Create following files in VScode to produce compile time, runtime and logical errors.

Disclaimer – While writing this book, we did use latest available version of Truffle i.e. v5.0.18 (core: 5.0.18) along with Node v12.2.0. Truffle v5.0.18 is using solc compiler version 0.5.0 and cannot compile code beyond 0.5.0. This is the reason of using pragma version "0.5.0" instead of "0.5.1".

Recipe that produces compile time error is below:

Contract1.sol

```
pragma solidity ^0.5.0;
contract Contract1 {
    //define mapping to store key-value pairs
    mapping(string => userRecord) userRecordMapping;
    //organize user records using struct
    struct userRecord
    {
        string unique_identification;
        string name;
        int age;
        bool is_smoke;
        bool is_consume_alcohol;
        int time_period;
        string add1;
        string add2;
        string add3;
        string phone;
        string fax;
        bool is_house_owner;
        bool is_farm_owner;
        bool is_pet_owner;
        bool is_businessman;
    }
```

//this method will throw "stack to deep" error due to more number of arguments in the function. If we remove one argument from this function then it will work just fine.

```
    function saveUserDetails(string memory unique_identification, int
age, string memory name, bool is_smoke, bool is_consume_alcohol, int
time_period,string memory add1, string memory add2, string memory
add3, string memory phone,string memory fax, bool is_house_owner, bool
is_farm_owner, bool is_pet_owner, bool is_businessman) public payable {
```

```
    userRecordMapping[unique_identification] = userRecord(unique_
identification, name, age, is_smoke, is_consume_alcohol, time_period,
add1, add2, add3, phone,fax, is_house_owner, is_farm_owner, is_pet_
owner, is_businessman);
    }
}
```

Recipe that produces run time error is below: In this case, ethereum EVM discards running of code.

Contract2.sol

```
pragma solidity ^0.5.0;
contract Contract2{
    string private value;
    //EVM rejects execution and returns out of gas message
    function method1(string memory _value) public{
        while(true){ //infinite loop exhausts gas
            value = _value;
        }
    }
}
```

Recipe that produces logical error is below: Here code crashes due to programming logic misses.

Contract3.sol

```
pragma solidity ^0.5.0;
contract Contract3{
    uint result;
    /*Results in "LogicalError. Divide error: VM error: invalid opcode" if
num1 is 0 i.e. Division by zero.
    */
    function divide(uint num, uint num1) public returns (uint) {
        result = num/num1;
        return result;
    }
}
```

To start debugging smart contracts using truffle, readers need to setup the truffle environment.

- Create a new folder "truffle-debug" inside

  "solidity_programming_practical_samples/Troubleshooting and Debugging".

  mkdir truffle-debug

  cd truffle-debug

- Initiate truffle project. This will create complete truffle project structure. You can find directories like "contracts" and "migrations" within project structure.

  truffle init

- Move all three contract files i.e Contract1.sol, Contract2.sol and Contract3.sol under "/contracts" folder inside "truffle-debug" project.

- Create a new file "2_deploy_contracts.js" inside "/migrations" folder under "truffle-debug" project. Code in this file allows readers to deploy contract files to ethereum blockchain network. Paste following code in file.

```
const CompileTimeError = artifacts.require("Contract1");
const RunTimeError = artifacts.require("Contract2");
const LogicalError = artifacts.require("Contract3");

module.exports = function(deployer) {
  deployer.deploy(CompileTimeError);
  deployer.deploy(RunTimeError);
  deployer.deploy(LogicalError);
```

- Open terminal (VScode Terminal-1) and go to "truffle-debug" project directory. Now compile smart contracts using following truffle command

- "truffle compile"

- You will get output as following.
  Compiling your contracts...

  ```
  =============================
  ```

  > Compiling.\contracts\Contract1.sol

  > Compiling.\contracts\Contract2.sol

  > Compiling.\contracts\Contract3.sol

  > Compiling.\contracts\Migrations.sol

  /XXX/truffle-debug/contracts/Contract1.sol:29:63:
  CompilerError: Stack too deep, try removing local variables.

  ... nique_identification] = userRecord(unique_identification,
  name, age, is_smoke, is_consume_a...

  ```
                  ^-------------------^
  ```

  Compilation failed. See above.

  Truffle v5.0.18 (core: 5.0.18)

  Node v12.2.0

  In above output, you can easily infer that our "Contract1.sol"
  file failed to compile due to error "CompilerError: Stack too
  deep, try removing local variables" as we had expected.

  To make this contract work, we will remove one argument
  from "saveUserDetails" method and "userRecord" struct (to
  match struct variable count) as compile time error is caused
  by exceeded number of arguments. Now our "Contract1.sol"
  should look like following contract and should not render
  previously seen compile time error.

```solidity
pragma solidity ^0.5.0;
contract UserRecordKeeper {
  //Define mapping to store key-value pairs
  mapping(string => userRecord) userRecordMapping;
  //Organize user records using struct
  struct userRecord
  {
      string unique_identification;
      string name;
      int age;
      bool is_smoke;
      bool is_consume_alcohol;
      int time_period;
      string add1;
      string add2;
      string add3;
      string phone;
      string fax;
      bool is_house_owner;
      bool is_farm_owner;
      bool is_pet_owner;
  }
```

//This method will throw "stack to deep" error.Because of more number of argument in function. If we remove one argument from function then it will work.

```solidity
  function saveUserDetails(string memory unique_identification, int
age, string memory name, bool is_smoke, bool is_consume_alcohol, int
time_period,string memory add1, string memory add2, string memory
add3, string memory phone,string memory fax, bool is_house_owner, bool
is_farm_owner, bool is_pet_owner) public payable  {
```

```
    userRecordMapping[unique_identification] = userRecord(unique_
identification, name, age, is_smoke, is_consume_alcohol, time_period,
add1, add2, add3, phone,fax, is_house_owner, is_farm_owner, is_pet_
owner);
  }
}
```

Now replace "Contract1.sol" code with "Contract1_rectified. sol" code.

- Try again to compile contracts using "truffle compile" command.

- Hurray, our contracts are compiled successfully.

- Here is the output.

Compiling your contracts...

============================

> Compiling.\contracts\Contract1.sol

> Compiling.\contracts\Contract2.sol

> Compiling.\contracts\Contract3.sol

> Compiling.\contracts\Migrations.sol

> Artifacts written to XXXX\truffle-debug\build\contracts

> Compiled successfully using: - solc: 0.5.0+commit.1d4f565a. Emscripten.clang

- Now it's time to deploy our contracts to blockchain network. We can start ethereum blockchain using ganache-cli. FYI..Ganache is part of truffle suite. Read more about ganache on its official site - https://truffleframework.com/ganache

Open a new terminal (VScode Terminal-2) and go to "truffle-debug" project directory. Thereafter execute command "ganache-cli". This will run ethereum blockchain with 10 default test accounts. You will witness output as follows:

```
Ganache CLI v6.4.3 (ganache-core: 2.5.5)

Available Accounts
==================
(0) 0x251ad351367ad1369024fdbdcf725bded293f3bf (~100 ETH)
(1) 0x1596a68d67e6d431f668fa8b75c7b64a23cd114b (~100 ETH)
(2) 0xb25a170ca524992ee80ce83415e8f7d72b70ecb6 (~100 ETH)
(3) 0xd4f92ebe5cfe1b36abd4fbff382de40c708ea2a1 (~100 ETH)
(4) 0x62403f3278483d34112c0f33f27fea665cb4f4c2 (~100 ETH)
(5) 0x9bcff945fbdaa7f358fb6acd384aed345883270a (~100 ETH)
(6) 0x541099940be60f734f2d21672e3ac041d88bf391 (~100 ETH)
(7) 0xff9ffeb0feb3e93538901bbc7f4f96b9bff26b57 (~100 ETH)
(8) 0xd5edb6b1ba6095b49712a807fe9ebf24c0b88f30 (~100 ETH)
(9) 0x85abef36635e63af8202cb7a8849f520d798867f (~100 ETH)

Private Keys
==================
(0) 0x5b93564eb8bcf96881a01f3b4281403b75d2671147f55aa1f4bc6e4749401bbf
(1) 0x3837f97ca67715e6cb534df531c1d5520694514cc16c9746daea8c9558458125
(2) 0x6ffcb5dd3713120e59d292d390e7b6a213b545c82373bc326651f5ca75ebb507
(3) 0xf94b2e0e8cd6fc5bae78f14a7b240ea60e47ef4e89d7eeedd0e646eeddbcda5f
(4) 0x0ed6a314e051e00bb870e9cfb1157c5fd86f28ebe87344092cedf2fdd96e4e04
(5) 0x98d2dff5f5ae4454c9ee86e5febe78f2b5fa7a7ac02d4cdb274b1aa2bc79412d
(6) 0x5f65d638a696b801fab18c46eaf552b010994efd615ad03e0181ef0d0adf6b83
(7) 0xe2a70bd8f714f114ead05d498fbc94be9ee469e06c9e973a702eee93a599ba12
(8) 0x7947de1ae3eac80ca59d460fc5e3be76c9155709060a4ff6ae8b93224550a80f
(9) 0xd0af5ead05f9ec5067a9b86a6cd323d4480b53daa078c29e4c1f7a6f024413d5

HD Wallet
```

- In this step, we will change the configuration file of truffle-debug project i.e "tuffle-config.js" for Windows and "truffle.js" for OS other than Windows. Paste following code snippet in truffle config file.

```
module.exports = {
 networks: {
  ganache: {
   host: "127.0.0.1",
   port: 8545,
   network_id: "*",
  },
  tenderly: {
```

```
        host: "127.0.0.1",
        port: 9545,
        network_id: "*",
        gasPrice: 0
      }
    },
  };
```

- Now it's time to deploy contracts on blockchain. To accomplish this, let's open a new terminal (VScode Terminal-3) and execute command "truffle migrate --network ganache". You will see output like this:

```
Deploying 'Contract1'
---------------------
> transaction hash:    0x398c313233069e0fcc5784ba84268fbbd42d267ceb622938d8cb5dbb9dc492d3
> Blocks: 0            Seconds: 0
> contract address:    0xb6fC86A38112Fd121D944ABA7E9d10A242597427
> block number:        3
> block timestamp:     1558900236
> account:             0x251AD351367ad1369024fDbdCF725bdED293F3bf
> balance:             99.98142298
> gas used:            601909
> gas price:           20 gwei
> value sent:          0 ETH
> total cost:          0.01203818 ETH


Deploying 'Contract2'
---------------------
> transaction hash:    0xe6fee6a0fdd3b1cbe0b0d309f1742f20042f7c2b7cabf7b6bc23de83af884ba9
> Blocks: 0            Seconds: 0
> contract address:    0x5bB016e24C1a35977dbf726708bD41cc70962785
> block number:        4
> block timestamp:     1558900236
> account:             0x251AD351367ad1369024fDbdCF725bdED293F3bf
> balance:             99.97762184
> gas used:            190057
> gas price:           20 gwei
> value sent:          0 ETH
> total cost:          0.00380114 ETH


Deploying 'Contract3'
---------------------
> transaction hash:    0xe2cb0e2e5b6623dd296e343887b0d89daa1c9ccf39aad67356f806feaf50328c
> Blocks: 0            Seconds: 0
> contract address:    0x82C83494d23B84E7f849930eDda40a26DE6D9c1E
> block number:        5
> block timestamp:     1558900236
> account:             0x251AD351367ad1369024fDbdCF725bdED293F3bf
> balance:             99.97535346
```

Congratulations!! We have deployed all of the contracts successfully on local blockchain.

- After deployment, let's try to interact with smart contracts in order to debug them. On same terminal (VScode Terminal-3) open truffle console using command "truffle console --network ganache".

XXXX\truffle-debug>truffle console --network ganache

truffle(ganache)>

On truffle console - Write following commands in given sequence:

Create contract1 instance

Get account to execute contract

Call method from contract using contract instance

truffle(ganache)> let instance = await Contract1.deployed()

truffle(ganache)> let accounts = await web3.eth.getAccounts()

truffle(ganache)> instance.saveUserDetails("a001",24,"John", true,true,20,"plot 1","street 1","OR,501098","0101010101","010 1010101",true,true,true, {from: accounts[0]})

- You will see output of last command as depicted below. Output itself demonstrates that there is no issue in executing our "contract1" contract on blockchain. Congratulations friends!

- Now let's try to execute "Contract2" code on blockchain.

  truffle(ganache)> let instance1 = await Contract2.deployed()

  truffle(ganache)> let accounts1 = await web3.eth.getAccounts()

  truffle(ganache)>   instance1.method1("value1",   {from: accounts1[0]})

  You will see output of last command as depicted below:

  ```
  truffle(ganache)> instance1.method1("value1", {from: accounts[0]})
  Thrown:
  Error: Returned error: VM Exception while processing transaction: out of gas
      at XMLHttpRequest. onHttpResponseEnd (C:\Users\raj.jha\AppData\Roaming\npm\node_modules\truffle\build\webpack:\~\xhr2-cookies\dist\xml-http-request.js:318:1)
      at XMLHttpRequest. setReadyState (C:\Users\raj.jha\AppData\Roaming\npm\node_modules\truffle\build\webpack:\~\xhr2-cookies\dist\xml-http-request.js:208:1)
      at XMLHttpRequestEventTarget.dispatchEvent (C:\Users\raj.jha\AppData\Roaming\npm\node_modules\truffle\build\webpack:\~\xhr2-cookies\dist\xml-http-request-event-target.js:34:1)
      at XMLHttpRequest.request.onreadystatechange (C:\Users\raj.jha\AppData\Roaming\npm\node_modules\truffle\build\webpack:\~\web3\~\web3-providers-http\src\index.js:96:1)
      at C:\Users\raj.jha\AppData\Roaming\npm\node_modules\truffle\build\webpack:\~\web3\~\truffle-provider\wrapper.js:112:1
      at C:\Users\raj.jha\AppData\Roaming\npm\node_modules\truffle\build\webpack:\~\web3-eth\~\web3-core-requestmanager\src\index.js:140:1
      at Object.ErrorResponse (C:\Users\raj.jha\AppData\Roaming\npm\node_modules\truffle\build\webpack:\~\web3-eth\~\web3-core-helpers\src\errors.js:29:1)
  truffle(ganache)>
  ```

- In addition - Have a look at Terminal-2 where "ganache-cli" is in action. You will find the log details as depicted below. Copy Transaction Id that will be used in next step.

  Transaction: 0xf425802868a5c000c3b7d7b938ecb5de6409e4 1955a715ee29a85d948d2124aa

  Gas usage: 6721975

  Block Number: 32

  ....

  Runtime Error: Out of Gas

- Above error is "Out of Gas"; which means code logic resulted in a state that crossed gas limit stipulation and EVM terminated the code execution abruptly. Let's debug our code to find-out root cause of this issue.

  On Terminal-3(truffle console) execute command "debug <Transaction Id>" Where <Transaction id> is transaction what we need to debug. In this case, id is the one we had copied in last step. You will see output as depicted below:

```
truffle(ganache)> debug 0xf425802868a5c000c3b7d7b938ecb5de6409e41955a715ee29a85d948d2124aa
Starting Truffle Debugger...
√ Compiling your contracts...
√ Gathering information about your project and the transaction...
Addresses affected:
 0x7c1c385CA978f2F71DB7db7C2e0ab5F9F7F00E2F - Contract2

Commands:
(enter) last command entered (step next)
(o) step over, (i) step into, (u) step out, (n) step next
(;) step instruction (include number to step multiple), (p) print instruction
(h) print this help, (q) quit, (r) reset
(t) load new transaction, (T) unload transaction
(b) add breakpoint, (B) remove breakpoint, (c) continue until breakpoint
(+) add watch expression (`+:<expr>`), (-) remove watch expression (-:<expr>)
(?) list existing watch expressions and breakpoints
(v) print variables and values, (:) evaluate expression - see `v`


Contract2.sol:

3: */
4: pragma solidity ^0.5.0;
5: contract Contract2{
   ^^^^^^^^^^^^^^^^^^^^^^^
```

- Keep pressing 'Enter' to continue debug the code in console. You will observe that every time "while(true)" statement repeats - This indicates there is some infinite loop caused by the statement.

- Good news - We have identified the line of code that caused the issue. Good Job!

```
function method1(string memory _value) public{
    while(true){ //Infinite loop cause out of gas.
      value = _value;
    }
}
```

- After finding the root cause, readers can fix the code as a next step. Let's fix Contract2.sol code for now by removing the "while(true)" loop from code. After this change, Contract2.sol will look like the one depicted below:

```
pragma solidity ^0.5.0;
contract Contract2{
    string private value;
    //EVM rejects execution and return out of gas.
    function method1(string memory _value) public{
        value = _value;
    }
}
```

- Exit debugger using command "q".

- Now let's migrate contract again. Use command "migrate --reset" on same terminal (VScode Terminal-3)

  truffle(ganache)> migrate –reset

- Then execute "Contract2" on blockchain with following command:

  truffle(ganache)> let instance1 = await Contract2.deployed()

  truffle(ganache)> let accounts1 = await web3.eth.getAccounts()

  truffle(ganache)>   instance1.method1("value1",   {from: accounts1[0]})

- Congratulations! We have executed "Contract2" successfully. You should see output as depicted below:

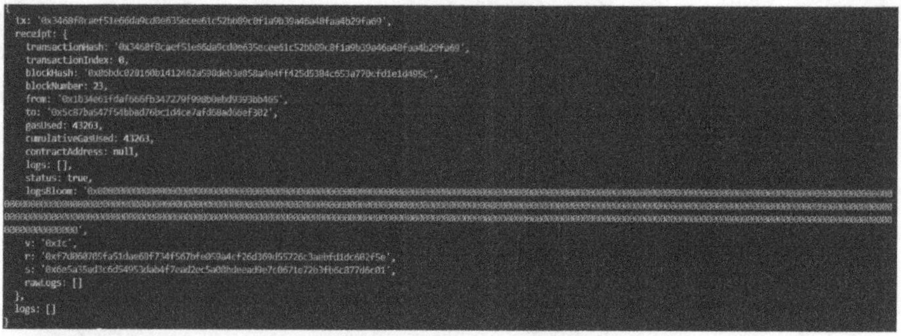

- Now it is time to execute last contract i.e "Contract3" on blockchain VScode Terminal-3.

truffle(ganache)> let instance3 = await Contract3.deployed()

truffle(ganache)> let accounts3 = await web3.eth.getAccounts()

truffle(ganache)> instance3. divide (10,0,{from: accounts3[0]})

- You will get runtime error "Error: Returned error: VM Exception while processing transaction: invalid opcode".

```
truffle(ganache)> instance3. divide (10,0, {from: accounts3[0]})
Thrown:
Error: Returned error: VM Exception while processing transaction: invalid opcode
    at XMLHttpRequest. onHttpResponseEnd (C:\Users\raj.jha\AppData\Roaming\npm\node_modules\truffle\build\webpack:\~\xhr2-cookies\dist\xml-http-request.js:318:1)
    at XMLHttpRequest. setReadyState (C:\Users\raj.jha\AppData\Roaming\npm\node_modules\truffle\build\webpack:\~\xhr2-cookies\dist\xml-http-request.js:208:1)
    at XMLHttpRequestEventTarget.dispatchEvent (C:\Users\raj.jha\AppData\Roaming\npm\node_modules\truffle\build\webpack:\~\xhr2-cookies\dist\xml-http-request-event-target.j
s:34:1)
    at XMLHttpRequest.request.onreadystatechange (C:\Users\raj.jha\AppData\Roaming\npm\node_modules\truffle\build\webpack:\~\web3\~\web3-providers-http\src\index.js:96:1)
    at C:\Users\raj.jha\AppData\Roaming\npm\node_modules\truffle\build\webpack:\packages\truffle-provider\wrapper.js:112:1
    at C:\Users\raj.jha\AppData\Roaming\npm\node_modules\truffle\build\webpack:\~\web3-eth\~\web3-core-requestmanager\src\index.js:140:1
    at Object.ErrorResponse (C:\Users\raj.jha\AppData\Roaming\npm\node_modules\truffle\build\webpack:\~\web3-eth\~\web3-core-helpers\src\errors.js:29:1)
truffle(ganache)>
```

- Copy <Transaction ID> from Terminal-2 (where we did initiate "ganache-cli") and debug it on Terminal-3(truffle console) with execute command "debug <Transaction ID>".

- You will get output as depicted below.

```
truffle(ganache)> debug 0x21a0e11cd6f013ff178660d33ce089094e92c3c05707f431a66c0f7c70c43563
Starting Truffle Debugger...
√ Compiling your contracts...
√ Gathering information about your project and the transaction...
Addresses affected:
  0x1EF6fb67333B3Aa9C9B72862dA3bBda721d08Cc6F - Contract3

Commands:
(enter) last command entered (step next)
(o) step over, (i) step into, (u) step out, (n) step next
(;) step instruction (include number to step multiple), (p) print instruction
(h) print this help, (q) quit, (r) reset
(t) load new transaction, (T) unload transaction
(b) add breakpoint, (B) remove breakpoint, (c) continue until breakpoint
(+) add watch expression ('+:<expr>'), (-) remove watch expression (-:<expr>)
(?) list existing watch expressions and breakpoints
(v) print variables and values, (:) evaluate expression - see `v`


Contract3.sol:

3: */
4: pragma solidity ^0.5.0;
5: contract Contract3{
   ^^^^^^^^^^^^^^^^^^^^^
```

- Press 'Enter' to go to next line on debugger window. Post few 'Enter' clicks, program will terminate abruptly where bug gets encountered.

```
debug(ganache:0x21a0e11c...)>
Contract3.sol:

9:      */
10:     function divide(uint num, uint num1) public returns (uint) {
11:         result = num/num1;
                       ^^^

debug(ganache:0x21a0e11c...)>
Contract3.sol:

9:      */
10:     function divide(uint num, uint num1) public returns (uint) {
11:         result = num/num1;
                   ^^^^^^^^^

debug(ganache:0x21a0e11c...)>

Transaction halted with a RUNTIME ERROR.

This is likely due to an intentional halting expression, like assert(), require() or revert(). It can also be due to out-of-gas exceptions. Please inspect your transaction
parameters and contract code to determine the meaning of this error.
debug(ganache:0x21a0e11c...)>
```

- With above debug process in action, we can easily find out the line of code that is causing havoc. In this case, the line in code causing trouble is:

  result = num/num1;

- We believe readers can easily comprehend - Division by zero is the root cause here. To fix this, we can place pertinent exceptional handling in code so that it does not fail execution anymore.

- There we go, we have debugged our Contract3.sol successfully!

Truffle comes readily shipped with in-built debugger. To debug solidity code with truffle debugger, we need to generate a transaction using solidity code and then use that <Transaction ID> to debug code using following command.

```
truffle(ganache)> debug 0x21a0e11cd6f013ff178660d33ce089094e92c3c05707f431a66c0f7c70c43563
Starting Truffle Debugger...
√ Compiling your contracts...
√ Gathering information about your project and the transaction...
Addresses affected:
 0x1EF6fb67338J4a9C9B72862dA3b8da721d08Cc6F - Contract3

Commands:
(enter) last command entered (step next)
(o) step over, (i) step into, (u) step out, (n) step next
(;) step instruction (include number to step multiple), (p) print instruction
(h) print this help, (q) quit, (r) reset
(t) load new transaction, (T) unload transaction
(b) add breakpoint, (B) remove breakpoint, (c) continue until breakpoint
(+) add watch expression (`+:<expr>`), (-) remove watch expression (-:<expr>)
(?) list existing watch expressions and breakpoints
(v) print variables and values, (:) evaluate expression - see `v`

Contract3.sol:

3: */
4: pragma solidity ^0.5.0;
5: contract Contract3{
   ^^^^^^^^^^^^^^^^^^^^
```

"debug <Transaction Id>" will open a user interface and allow usage of debugger features that include evaluate expressions, inspect Solidity variables and set breakpoints to help debugging contract code.

Here is a list of commands that complements debugger features efficiently.

Command	Use	Command	Use
enter	Step Next	u	Step Out
o	Step Over	n	Step Next
i	Step Into	;	Step Multiple
u	Step Out	p	Print Instruction
h	Help	q	Quit
r	Reset	t	Load new Transaction
T	Load Transaction	b	Add Breakpoint
B	Remove Breakpoint	c	Continue Until Breakpoint
?	List Watch Expressions and Breakpoints	v	Print Variables and Values
+<exp>	Add Watch Expression	-<exp>	Remove Watch Expression

Internally, truffle debugger interacts with Ethereum client (ganache-cli in our case) to collect all the data needed to debug code and stores data in Redux store. Note: Data includes contract bytecode, contract code abstract representations and instructions that generated transaction of code so on and so forth.

Additional Context

Remix online editor also encompasses debugging tool with multiple features. Let's debug Contract3.sol using it to understand it's working.

- Open https://remix.ethereum.org. Create a new.sol file. Copy recipe code from VScode file "Contract3.sol" and paste it into remix.sol file.

- Go to 'Run' tab on top right section.

- Inside 'Run' choose environment in the dropdown to 'JavaScript VM' and deploy code. Try to execute "divide" method with argument (10,0).

- See screenshot below:

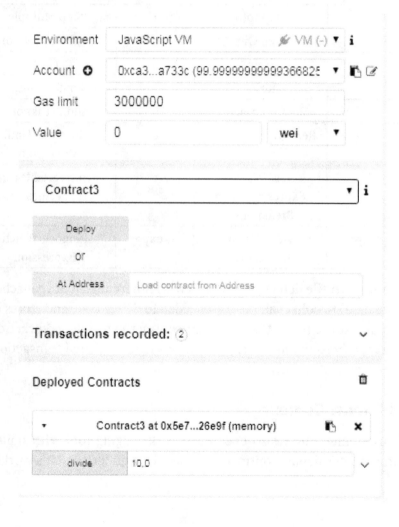

- Execution of "divide" method will render an error and produce error log in Remix console as depicted below:

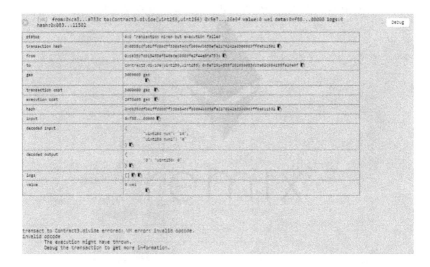

- You can start debugging code by pressing "Debug" button within error console to eventually find "Debugger" tab window. Alternatively, you can copy "transaction hash" from console and then use "Debugger" tab to paste copied transaction hash in the "transaction index or hash" text box. Thereafter press "start debugging" button. See screenshot below:

- Step over forward multiple times using "step over forward" button from following pallet. This pallet has many feature buttons to support many debugging options.

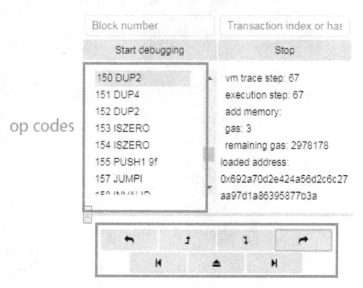

- Multiple clicks of "Step over forward" will take you through different breakpoints and you can observe changing opcodes section in action on real time (look at screenshot above). Soon you will reach line of code that caused "Invalid Opcode" error. See screenshot below:

- Hurray! We have successfully debugged our Contract3.sol code on Remix as well.

Go through official Remix document to understand more details on debugging processes and related terminologies: https://remix. readthedocs.io/en/latest/tutorial_debug.html.

Exception and Error Handling

Introduction

EVM is a world state machine that treats transaction as an atomic operation that should be all complete OR do nothing (zero effect). In the same note, Solidity exceptions also result in revert of state when error is encountered amidst transaction execution. This can undo all the state changes in current call or its inner calls. This also complements an error flag to caller.

With release of version 0.4.10, solidity introduced require(), assert() and revert() functions for error and exception handling. Require() and revert() refund any left-over gas in case exception occurs while assert() consumes all the gas. Thus we have to be very careful when we are using assert(). We will understand the scenarios and recommendations with our recipe code examples. Stay tuned!

Pre Deep Dive Considerations

- Launch VS code editor to write or edit code.

- Create a new folder inside folder 'solidity_programming_ practical_samples' and name it "Troubleshooting and Debugging".

- Open Remix online editor on browser to compile and run the recipe code.

- In next section we will be enhancing one of the erstwhile contract "function_external_call.sol" that we had developed in previous chapters.

```solidity
pragma solidity ^0.5.1;
// No exception handling has been done here. Code is just for quick
demonstration.
//Insurance company contract that calculates insurance premium based
on age, time duration, alcohol consumption status and smoking habit
affirmation
contract InsurerCompany {
    //Infinite method has defined payable only because we can show how
we can pass gas while calling it.
    function insuranceAmountCalculator(int age,bool is_smoke, bool
is_consume_alcohol,int time_period) external payable returns (int
insurance_amount) {
        int variable_amount = 0;
        if(is_consume_alcohol){
            variable_amount = variable_amount + 100;
        }
        if(is_smoke){
            variable_amount = variable_amount + 100;
        }
        return ((variable_amount + (age + 50)) - time_period); //Random
logic to calculate insurance premium based on age, time duration, alcohol
consumption status and smoking habit affirmation
    }

}


//Contract for insurance agent. Insurance agent saving client user info and
calculate insurance premium using Insurer company contract.
contract InsuranceAgent {
    InsurerCompany ic;
    constructor(address _ic) public {
        ic = InsurerCompany(_ic); //assuming we know address of
InsurerCompany contract. Initialize third party contract in constructor.
    }
```

```solidity
//Define mapping to store key-value pairs.
mapping(string => userRecord) userRecordMapping;

//Organize user records using struct
struct userRecord
{
    string unique_identification;
    string name;
    int age;
    bool is_smoke;
    bool is_consume_alcohol;
    int time_period;
}
//Save user record. Test data to test on Remix - ("U123",20,"Jon",true,true,10)
function saveUserDetails(string memory unique_identification, int age,
string memory name, bool is_smoke, bool is_consume_alcohol, int time_
period) public payable {
    userRecordMapping[unique_identification] = userRecord(unique_
identification, name, age, is_smoke, is_consume_alcohol, time_period);
}

//Retrieve insurance premium information using third party contract.
Test data to test on Remix - ("U123")
function getInsurancePremium(string memory unique_identification)
public payable returns (int){
    /*
    value(msg.value) - send gas in wei unit to destination contract i.e
InsurerCompany.
    gas(1000) - Set gas limit modifier.
    */
    return ic.insuranceAmountCalculator.value(msg.value).
gas(1000)(userRecordMapping[unique_identification].
age, userRecordMapping[unique_identification].is_smoke,
userRecordMapping[unique_identification].is_consume_alcohol,
userRecordMapping[unique_identification].time_period);
}
}
```

We will add errors and exception handling in this erstwhile code.

Code Recipes for Practical Learning

Create following files in VScode. "exception_error_handling.sol" to comprehend exception and error handling using "require", "revert" and "assert". Paste following code snippet in this file:

```solidity
pragma solidity ^0.5.1;
// Some exception handling has been done now however code is just for
quick demonstration.
//Contract logic to calculate insurance premium based on age, time
duration, alcohol consumption status and smoking habit affirmation
contract InsurerCompany {
    //This method has defined payable only because we can show how we
can pass gas while calling it.
    function insuranceAmountCalculator(int age,bool is_smoke, bool
is_consume_alcohol,int time_period) external payable returns (int
insurance_amount) {
        int variable_amount = 0;
        require(age >= 0, "age should be non zero.");
        require(time_period >= 0, "time period should be non-zero.");

        if(is_consume_alcohol){
            variable_amount = variable_amount + 100;
        }
        if(is_smoke){
            variable_amount = variable_amount + 100;
        }
        return ((variable_amount + (age + 50)) - time_period); //Random
logic to calculate insurance premium based on age, time duration, alcohol
consumption status and smoking habit affirmation
    }
}
```

```solidity
//Contract for insurance agent. Insurance agent saving client user info and
calculate insurance premium using Insurer company contract.
contract InsuranceAgent {
    InsurerCompany ic;
    constructor(address _ic) public {
        ic = InsurerCompany(_ic); //Assuming we know address of
InsurerCompany contract. Initialize third party contract in constructor.
    }
    //Define mapping to store key-value pairs.
    mapping(string => userRecord) userRecordMapping;
    //Organize user records using struct
    struct userRecord
    {
        string unique_identification;
        string name;
        int age;
        bool is_smoke;
        bool is_consume_alcohol;
        int time_period;
        bool is_insured;
        int premium_amount;
        uint commence_timestamp;
        bool claim_settlement_done;
    }
    //Save user record. Test data to test on Remix -
("U123",20,"Jon",true,true,10,false)
    function saveUserDetails(string memory unique_identification, int age,
string memory name, bool is_smoke, bool is_consume_alcohol, int time_
period, bool claim_settlement_done) public payable {
        //User input error and exception handling
        require(age >= 0, "age should be non zero.");
        require(time_period >= 0, "time period should be non-zero.");
        require(claim_settlement_done == false,"claim settlement flag should
save with false");
```

```
    bool is_insured = false; //Should be zero while user registration
    int premium_amount = 0; //Should be zero while user registration
    uint commence_timestamp = block.timestamp; //Timestamp of
insurance commence

    userRecordMapping[unique_identification] = userRecord(unique_
identification, name, age, is_smoke, is_consume_alcohol, time_period,
is_insured, premium_amount, commence_timestamp, claim_settlement_
done);
    }


    //Retrieve insurance premium information using third party contract.
Test data to test on Remix - ("U123")
    function getInsurancePremium(string memory unique_identification)
public payable returns (int){
        /*
        value(msg.value) - send gas in wei unit to destination contract i.e
InsurerCompany.
        gas(1000) - Set gas limit modifier.
        */
        return ic.insuranceAmountCalculator.value(msg.value).
gas(1000)(userRecordMapping[unique_identification].
age, userRecordMapping[unique_identification].is_smoke,
userRecordMapping[unique_identification].is_consume_alcohol,
userRecordMapping[unique_identification].time_period);
    }


    //Test data to test on Remix - ("U123")
    function doInsurance(string memory unique_identification) public
payable{
        userRecordMapping[unique_identification].is_insured = true;
        userRecordMapping[unique_identification].premium_amount =
getInsurancePremium(unique_identification);
    }

    //Test data to test on Remix - ("U123",true,true)
```

```
function claimInsurance(string memory unique_identification, bool
is_smoke, bool is_consume_alcohol) public payable {
    if(is_smoke != userRecordMapping[unique_identification].is_smoke
|| is_consume_alcohol != userRecordMapping[unique_identification].
is_consume_alcohol){
        revert("Provided information while claim is different from our
recorded information that we got while registering for insurance.");
    }
    assert(userRecordMapping[unique_identification].claim_settlement_
done != true); //If already claimed before then lose all gas as penalty
    /*
    Pertinent claim process will execute here such as transfer claim
amount to claimant's account.
    */
    userRecordMapping[unique_identification].claim_settlement_done =
true; //Congratulation friends. Claim settlement is complete successfully.
    }
}
```

In our recipe, we have two contracts "InsurerCompany" and "InsuranceAgent". InsuranceAgent is bridge between customer and InsurerCompany. Customers are using "InsuranceAgent" methods to fulfill its insurance needs. Let's ponder over a pertinent use-case:

- Customer can provide personal information to InsuranceAgent to be saved to blockchain. InsuranceAgent will do error and exception handling against customer provided data.

- Customer can get insurance through InsuranceAgent. InsuranceAgent retrieves insurance premium amount from InsurerCompany.

- Customer can claim insurance and ask for settlement through InsuranceAgent. Customer has to provide supporting data required for claim settlement basis laid guideline.

- If customer provided data is correct and validations are valid then claim settlement takes place seamlessly.

- Customer will lose gas amount if already claimed insurance is re-attempted.

Run on Remix Online Editor

To perform recipe easily on remix, please follow below steps. Going through comments inside code snippet is equally important here so please do not overlook them.

1. Open https://remix.ethereum.org. Create a new.sol file. Copy recipe code from your VScode file "exception_error_handling. sol" and paste it on remix.sol file.

2. Go to 'Run' tab on top right section.

3. Inside 'Run' choose environment in the dropdown to 'JavaScript VM'.

4. You will see two contract names in the dropdown inside deploy section. These contracts are "InsurerCompany" and "InsuranceAgent". See screenshot below to get more clarity and complete context:

5. Note: Deployment order of contracts is very important as we are using deploy address of "InsurerCompany" in constructor while deploying "InsuranceAgent". As a result, "InsurerCompany" should be deployed beforehand. Choose "InsurerCompany" option from dropdown and deploy it. After deployment, copy the address of deployed contract. Refer screenshot below for your ready reference:

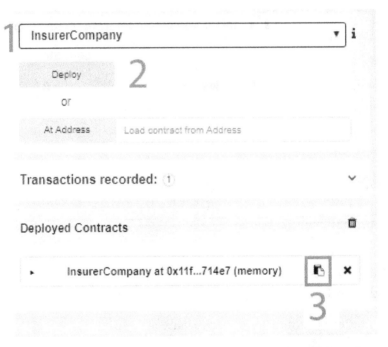

Thereafter choose "InsuranceAgent" contract from dropdown and deploy it with address that you copied in last step.

6. Subsequently execute methods available in contract in following order

    "saveUserDetails()" => "doInsurance()" => "claimInsurance()"

    See screenshot below:

Until now, we have used user provided arguments that results in no exception or error. We will now play with arguments to test error and exception handling code.

Solidity uses "assert" and "require" functions to validate conditions. Exception is triggered if any condition is not satisfied. "revert()" however is not using any conditional statement as depicted below:

require(<condition>, <error message>)

assert(<condition>, <error message>)

revert(<error message>)

Require vs Revert

See our contract code below where we are validating the user input using "require" and throw exception in contract methods "saveUserDetails" and "insuranceAmountCalculator".

```
//User input error and exception handling
    require(age >= 0, "age should be non zero.");
    require(time_period >= 0, "time period should be non-zero.");
    require(claim_settlement_done == false, "claim settlement flag should
save with false");
```

Contract methods are expecting age and time_period arguments as positive number and claim_settlement_done field as false. If user inputs do not meet these conditions, then code should raise exception.

Let's execute our contract method "saveUserDetails" with user arguments that are not congruent with contract expectations. User supplied age variable is a negative number i.e "-20". You will get exception as depicted below on Remix console.

"require()" and "revert()" work in similar fashion and refund left over gas that remain unused in transactions. "require" is using "0xfd" opcode which is mapped to "REVERT" instruction on ethereum EVM. This means, when "require()" throws exception it should be identified by EVM as REVERT instruction. To understand this see the last screenshot where "require(age >= 0, "age should be non-zero.");" statement has raised error but you will find "REVERT" instruction on Remix console (highlighted in screenshot).

We use "require()" more often, exceptions are only those scenarios where in condition statements, we need to implement complex business logic. In our code snippet we have used revert() just for demonstration.

```
if(is_smoke != userRecordMapping[unique_identification].is_smoke
|| is_consume_alcohol != userRecordMapping[unique_identification].
is_consume_alcohol){
        revert("Provided information while claim is different from our
recorded information that we received while registering for insurance.");
    }
```

Assert:

As we mentioned before "assert()" consumes all the gas amount when exception/error occurs. Practically any appropriately functioning code should never encounter "assert()". Hence we should use "assert()" only in those conditions where we never expect our contract to fail. In our code example we used "assert()" once when we try to re-claim an insurance after claiming it already[Cheating or Ignorance – Do not know really ☺].

```
assert(userRecordMapping[unique_identification].claim_settlement_done
!= true); //if already claimed before then lose all gas (Penalty)
```

Let us execute our recipe again on Remix editor and try to raise exception using assert. In our contract if user tried to reclaim an already claimed insurance then "assert()" will execute. On Remix try to call function "claimInsurance()" again to reclaim insurance. You will get following exception.

There is one catch here, exception raised by "assert()" is not identified by EVM and hence EVM throw "invalid opcode" error. This is because "assert()" used 0xfe opcode which is not recognized by ethereum EVM as yet.

Additional Context

There are more best practices while using assert(), require() and revert(). These practices are not standard protocols and can vary based on experience and expertise of smart contract developers. Some of these are:

- Require() should be used in beginning of the method.

- Require() is used to validate response data coming from external contracts. As we did emulate in our contract where "InsurerCompany" contract is validating age and time_period data that is coming from external contract i.e "InsuranceAgent".

```
contract InsurerCompany {
    function insuranceAmountCalculator(int age,bool is_smoke, bool
is_consume_alcohol,int time_period) external payable returns (int
insurance_amount) {

        ........................
        require(age >= 0, "age should be non zero.");
        require(time_period >= 0, "time period should be non-zero.");


        ........................
    }
}

contract InsuranceAgent {
    InsurerCompany ic;
    constructor(address _ic) public {
```

```
      ic = InsurerCompany(_ic); //Assuming we know address of
InsurerCompany contract. Initialize third party contract in constructor.
   }

......................................................
   function getInsurancePremium(string memory unique_identification)
public payable returns (int){
      /*
      value(msg.value) - send gas in wei unit to destination contract i.e
InsurerCompany.
      gas(1000) - Set gas limit modifier.
      */
      return ic.insuranceAmountCalculator.value(msg.value).
gas(1000)(userRecordMapping[unique_identification].
age, userRecordMapping[unique_identification].is_smoke,
userRecordMapping[unique_identification].is_consume_alcohol,
userRecordMapping[unique_identification].time_period);
   }

......................................................
}
```

- Assert() should be used towards end of method.

- Assert() will check invariants in contract.

Summary:

After developing code, the next logical step is to test it thoroughly to ascertain whether the code produces expected output or not. Debugging and troubleshooting are step by step processes of detecting errors and corresponding resolution. As developers we all come across many unwanted situations hence knowing best practices and right techniques equip us to deal with them and helps produce high quality in the end. Learnings in this chapter are vital tools for readers in dealing with diverse smart contract issues. It is vital to follow the learnings to produce quality results. That said, find your own subtle ways to deal with issues by honing your skills continuously. All the best in your endeavour and quest towards highest quality contracts.

CHAPTER 8

Futuristic Considerations

Security and Privacy Principle When Blockchain Meets with IOT

IoT has vast landscape and prospect in verticals such as smart infrastructure, healthcare, agriculture and smart devices to name a few. Users have enormous data with them, and they are geared up to upload their data for wider use, as a result, huge number of discrete data points get engraved every day passing by. Risk of hijacking data, privacy vulnerabilities, disruption to business operations and inhibitions to internet enabled services due to large-scale distributed denial-of-service attacks make IoT insecure and untrustworthy.

IoT plays crucial role in transforming cities into smart cities, grids into smart grids and vehicles into smart vehicles. Number of connected devices is estimated to reach between 30 and 40 billion in few years. Vulnerabilities to IoT are multifarious thus instituting insightful security mechanism is extremely vital. IoT works on Bring Your Own Device principle. Embedded devices have specialized operating systems, which are inhibited by memory and computing resources, making them diverge from traditional computing devices. These devices cannot capture complex encryption logic hence old-fashioned security systems is not the answer.

IoT Blockchain Integration

As part of ultramodern solutions, Blockchain and IoT are destined to come together under one parasol. IoT is based on the core idea of being able to make right choices at right time enabling stellar customer experience. Blockchain has ability to make IoT network distributed or decentralized having no single point of failure making it a huge complementary tool. This restricts malicious hacking of even a single IoT device. Blockchain enables consensus mechanism among IoT nodes and empowers them to verify decisions in-group. This establishes mechanism to find odd performing devices from network and potentially isolate them on real-time. Blockchain diminishes the risk of disseminated denial-of-service (DDoS) attacks that affect multiple devices at once based on non-contagious principle i.e. outage in one device can't effect other connected devices in the network.

Security Challenge in IoT and Blockchain Integration

To expedite the prospect, security in this integration needs special attention. This is essential to be an implementer in millions of IoT devices where transaction rate is extremely vital. Scaling challenge is being addressed by introducing concepts such as ZK-SNARK, Raiden, Sharding, Plasma and Lightning. In addition, security needs special attention to tap full potential of this integration.

IoT and Blockchain Platform Integration

Here is one of the blockchain and IoT integration architecture practiced widely. There is an integral platform that acts as a bridge between IoT events and blockchain ledger. This platform processes IoT data rapidly and identifies insights pertaining to IoT device behavior and triggered events. This also visualizes IoT data for structured execution. Blockchain in turn enhances trust and transparency by making IoT devices to corroborate various events in its hallmark immutable ledger.

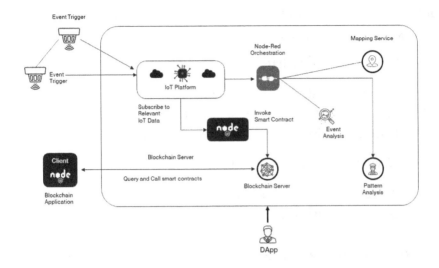

BlockChain requires a consensus algorithm to ensure agreement on identification and verification in a distributed system. The traditional blockchain employed in Bitcoin is costly due to the involvement of crypto puzzle solving process. Moreover, it requires computation power at a massive scale. As a result, traditional blockchain is suitable for distributed networks whereas it requires a consensus algorithm to ensure agreement on identification and verification in a distributed system. Its employment for mass adoption however requires a concrete solution. Let's explore some of the possibilities in the next section.

Futuristic Approach

Futuristic approach is exciting as it will curtail the need of a platform to integrate IoT events and blockchain ledger. In future, IoT devices will come dispatched with blockchain at its core thereby forming a sophisticated network of devices that can communicate to each other leveraging blockchain features without compromising the security. Acclimatizing blockchain with IoT requires to overcome one more fundamental issue of applying it in a constrained IoT computing as it requires well configured computing resources. Such adaption at a massive scale will require amendment in the model to make it indispensable IoT ecosystems keeping device cost as low as possible by adopting a lightweight architecture to enhance the computing power of devices. This will see the day of light by usage of:

- Thin client blockchain implementation

- Adopting out-of-the-box consensus mechanisms thereby eliminating the overheads of traditional blockchain while maintaining its security and privacy benefit

- Having blockchain installed in the IoT devices in a much leaner way

This network of smart IoT-Blockchain devices will transmute enterprise solutions to a level that is not less than a revolution.

Security Against Future Advanced Computing Strategies

Quantum computer is a big leap into future that uses quantum mechanics to deliver enormous processing power compared to erstwhile computing mechanisms. Quantum machines promise computing power not seen before. Current set of computers use pulsations representing everything into 1s or 0s. Everything from text, songs, videos so on and so forth are essentially strings of these binary digits. Quantum computers use qubits; which are typically subatomic particles such as electrons or photons. Managing qubits is huge engineering problem hence it is taking substantially more time to see quantum computers in real action. Researchers are using superconducting circuits cooled to low temperatures while few others are using electromagnetic fields on a silicon chip in vacuum chambers. In both the scenarios, the goal is to isolate the qubits in a meticulously maintained quantum state. Results are expected to be astonishing leading to a revolution not seen before. Quantum computer can solve complex mathematical calculations and algorithms that is demonstrably beyond the reach of even the most powerful supercomputers under the sun.

How does it Impact Blockchain

One of the vital building blocks of blockchain security mainly revolves around one-way mathematical functions. Researchers have used combinations of these functions in such a profound way that traditional computers can't reverse engineer them hence blockchain is very difficult to penetrate. These functions are used in digital signatures that blockchain uses for authentication. Hash consisting of bits is derived from a combination of existing ledger, reference to previous block and block that is to be added on the ledger. Every single addition or change alters its configuration. This is rather straightforward to find hash of a block but challenging to find a block that can yield a specific hash due to huge computing power needed to do reverse engineering. Today's computers can't use brute force to decode this in a reasonable time.

Quantum computers will pose a threat on this fundamental security principle and consideration as futuristic computers will be able to calculate one-way functions as it can use way more brute force to find the answers. Extensively used one-way encryption can potentially become useless and blockchain claim of zero security tolerance will become vulnerable. This can endanger the benefits it brings on the table. Hash, digital signatures, private-public keys and decentralized identity are key areas where breach can potentially take place. Being reactive can compromise security. If your private keys or digital signatures are stolen, it is devastating.

What is the Solution?

Devil can also become a savior. Quantum computing that poses threat is also the answer in the form of quantum cryptography that can replace traditional digital signatures. This requires protocol level changes that requires massive effort. Existing protocols needs each node in the network to be connected through traditional channels. Protocols will need massive changes to enable quantum cryptography in the blockchain world.

One-way functions need to be combined with complex algorithms keeping in mind quantum computing impact years down the line. Erstwhile blockchain platforms should become so capable of changing cryptographic algorithms to surprise future technology by being innovative. Researchers have a task in hand to devise ways to move away from traditional functions and find ways in next few years to make security intact so that quantum computers don't create havoc.

Scaling with Future Consensus Mechanisms and Solutions

Most commonly used consensus mechanism in today's age is proof of work. The speed of consensus impacts output significantly. Proof of Work involves extensive computation and resources. Block difficulty gets steeper with scale that requires more time and resources to process a transaction. There are many consensus mechanisms being pondered in various blockchain technologies. Proof of Work needs to phase out over time as blockchain attains maturity and endurance to scale up.

Alternative Mechanisms

Proof-of-Stake

One of the famous consensus technique is Proof of Stake. In fact, proof of stake is one of the most credible alternative emerged. In Proof of Stake, the miners put their standing at stake to validate a transaction. The algorithm randomly selects validators for block creation ensuring no validator can predict its turn proactively. The validators then get the reward for validating and processing the transaction. On a flip side, they lose stake in case of failure to validate a transaction.

Compared to Proof of Work, Proof of Stake is way more workable. PoS will also result in an improved occurrence of block addition since miners don't have to spend time solving the cryptographic puzzles. Tokens are more consistently distributed thus it provides more conclusiveness. There are few limitations with this mechanism and there are many variations of it being researched upon in recent times.

Delegated Proof-of-Stake

Although names are alike however this model is very different from Proof-of-stake model. In this consensus model, cryptocurrency owners do not include themselves in the decision making in any way. They vote in proportional to their stake. They elect delegates who represent them to undertake validation on their behalf. Elected delegates get shuffled sporadically to avoid any conflict of interest. Delegated Proof-of-Stake strikes balance between performance and decentralization.

Proof-of-Weight

This consensus algorithm has bendable options to substantiate stake of nodes. Traditionally, value of stake or standing is compared however in this model, any other parameter can be used as agreed among all. For examples: IPFS data stored by the node or the computation power comparison can get the miner elected to mine the block.

Proof-of-Authority

Proof-of-Authority is a consensus algorithm where transactions are validated by individual accounts validated by the administrator. Model allows participants to verify their individual identity and in turn earn privilege to validate the network. Process followed by administrator to select participants is based on a well-established structured process. Selected participants are the sole authority and other nodes depend on them to authenticate source of truth.

Proof-of-Burn

In this model, miners burn sun of cryptocurrency and earn a lifetime worth privilege to mine. The more the cryptocurrency is burnt, chances to get selected to mine block is more however the selection process is indiscriminate. Burning more cryptocurrency is the only way to increase your chances of being selected for mining. This model is very costly as resources are burnt to earn returns.

Proof-of-Elapsed-Time

This model saves substantial computing power. Each participating node in the network is required to wait till randomly decided time.

Nodes generate a random wait time and then go in sleep mode for that duration. Node waking up before other nodes is the one that has shortest elapsed time hence is given first opportunity to add a new block. System ensures the selection of wait time by nodes is random and can't be compromised.

Proof-of-Capacity

In Proof-of-Work miners change a number in the block header as fast as they can to ascertain a correct hash value. The first miner to identify correct hash value gets opportunity to validate. Proof-of-capacity enables nodes to use available space on their hard drive to compete against other nodes. More the possible outcome one can store on the hard drive, more the probability of a miner emerging as a winner.

Byzantine Fault Tolerance

Distributed network can potentially collapse if nodes do not agree on a common protocol to exchange information. Blockchain has no central authority hence this problem can cause a massive issue. The problem is explained in a famous paper where several Byzantine generals and their army have surrounded a city. They have two choices i.e. to attack or not to attack. Lack of congruence can become dangerous and result in commotion. Communication is not straight forward among them. Byzantine fault tolerance can help solve the problem. In this model, transactions reach the validating generals at dissimilar time and they react based on internal state maintained by them. Consensus is determined based on the collaborative decision submitted by generals.

Other scaling solutions are below:

1. Infrastructure:

Infrastructure guidelines to qualify for a node are not in place. The number of transactions blockchain can deliver can never exceed that of a single node that is participating in network. If all nodes are having high end and optimized servers as their strength, it can be a big plus in the scalability.

2. Sharding:

Sharding in the blockchain is alike database sharding used in traditional solutions. In databases, a shard is a horizontal partition of data in the database. Each shard is stored on a distinct database server. This enables spreading the load across servers. Similarly in blockchain world, Sharding will enable complete state of the blockchain set apart into numerous shards. Overall state gets split into smaller units and each unit in turn is stored by different nodes in the network. Transactions on the network are load balanced to different nodes conditional to the shard they epitomize.

3. NoN [Network of Network]:

In Agile, there is a prominent concept named Scrum of Scrum. Similarly Blockchain can devise NoN [Network of Network] concept by keeping a limit on nodes a network can accommodate. Beyond this, blocks of transactions will get recorded and validated on alternate network. A dependable and profligate mechanism needs to be developed to interchange information among networks. This solution can increase the transaction rate exponentially due to parallel processing.

4. Lightning:

The Lightning network objective is to make smart contract execution off blockchain for lower cost and way faster speed of transactions. Creation of a channel that represents a smart contract is of prime importance. This enhances speediness of transaction as majority of transactions are processed off chain.

Raiden is topology of Lightning on the Ethereum platform. Raiden Network boasts of Ethereum scalability to one million transactions per second. Raiden uses any ERC20-compliant token rather than just one currency.

5. Plasma:

Plasma is a scaling solution that uses child chains reporting into root chains to surge transaction rate without compromising security.

Here are its building blocks:

Client — Watches Ethereum and runs the child chain. Detects fraudulent behavior as soon as possible and exiting as desirable.

Child chain — Watches Ethereum for deposits and performs all computations vis-à-vis current state.

Root chain — Anchors child chains via smart contracts. Handles deposits and exits for a child chain, receiving only sufficient information to process both and to confirm or deny fraudulent exits.

Parent chain — Secures a child chain. Identical with root chain for the MVP. In Plasma's final form there can be numerous parent chains between a child chain and the root chain.

In the working Plasma chain, users need to move their assets from a parent chain to the child chain. To perform a deposit, users move assets from a parent chain to a child chain by transferring them to the appropriate smart contract on Ethereum. If an invalid transaction is included in the child chain, everyone must exit the child chain instantaneously. The child chain relies on block confirmations resulting in huge improvement in the scalability.

6. Concurrent Platform:

This approach addresses the problem at the fundamental level. Using base platform based on functional programming languages rather than traditional programming languages widely used as the underneath platform. Functional programming languages are much faster than customary languages for data analysis and processing. These are apt to leverage parallel processing and can fundamentally change the paradigm due to huge focus on multithreading.

That said – There are several more solutions being researched. Enhancing scalability will bring a huge up stick to blockchain. One of the above approaches or possibly combination of them may eventually bring blockchain scalability in the league of topmost bracket.

Advanced Privacy Rules

Blockchain privacy poisoning is a new term doing the rounds off late. This means personal data stored by blockchain will become noncompliant with privacy laws. In quest to become highly secure, blockchain technology has gone all out fundamentally on immutability as a result, public blockchains require an immutable data structure hence recorded data cannot be modified or deleted straightforwardly. Many privacy rule are binding around the globe where user data must be deleted within stipulation. Blockchain can be accused of privacy violation as this is not straightforward in this technology. Organizations employing blockchain without giving heed to privacy issues will run the caveat of keeping personal data leading to a tough situation. Current focus of this technology is getting acceptability in the enterprise world however overlooking privacy rules can prove fatal. To comply with privacy laws, blockchain can store personal data outside the boundary thereby meeting privacy laws at the first place. Secondly it can have a fundamental solution in place that allows deletion of private data with a structured and scientific model that can be emulated in tandem.

There is another significant problem at hand i.e. technology doesn't actually curtail digital privacy. The portals users visit, the applications they download, the shopping they do, services they use and many more are integral part of the world today. In today's jet age and constraints, these can be effortlessly exploitable and make users feel susceptible to data embezzlement. Best and optimal solution is to move forward with impartial decentralized networks where our intrinsic choices drive how information flow and storage can take place. The superlative solution shall put privacy at the forefront allowing users to communicate without restrictions, without any fear of corollary with trust that is synonymous to blockchain.

Problem is even more compound where some data pertaining to users can't be exposed directly on decentralized networks for mining the cryptocurrency. Here the nodes operating with the data can fork a new version of the blockchain intermittently thereby imitating requests for adaptation or elimination as deemed fit based on business need and privacy laws.

Privacy laws differ from one region to another hence there is need of a larger attempt to view the problem from a holistic perspective, get solutions deliberated and agreed with regulators beforehand to avoid risks in the long run. This is in the best interest of blockchain technology to be a cynosure technology.

Blockchain Future

What to expect in the coming time:

1. **Beyond Panacea Syndrome:** Blockchain hype did make entire world believe this technology is a panacea that will curtail all the problems that exist on the planet; which is untrue. Blockchain has its own set of issues. Impact it will bring is enormous however it does not fit the bill in every problem-statement. In the coming time, we will see practical methodology and pragmatic solutions around this technology as there is way more clarity on its usage and benefits than ever before. It will not be run of the mill kind of situation any longer rather diverse solutions that improve trust among transacting entities will be the driving force. This is the most critical sweet-spot of this technology hence should be garnished.

2. **Golden Triangle:** Primary stumbling block is the inequity among security, scalability and decentralization. Broader acceptance requires scrupulous equilibrium among these three to get best of both the world benefits. Researchers around the globe are working towards realizing scalability while conserving security and decentralization. Numerous solutions are on the prospect that will be game changer and permeate positivity in apprehending the true potential this technology can bring.

3. Finance, Supply-Chain, Logistics, Cyber Security and Healthcare will be Frontrunner: Blockchain will touch extensive areas however these will take lead in the mass adoption due to huge benefits blockchain carries. Groundwork is already in place in these and blockchain has been an important fragment of research in others. It's time to give elevation to it and adopt this technology with heart and soul.

4. Blockchain conjunction with IoT and AI: Blockchain, IoT and AI partnership is extremely vital. IoT and AI needs blockchain to reap opportunity that IoT, AI and blockchain represent. With solutions around scalability and interoperability on the horizon, world will observe huge introduction of their amalgamation. Together they will form a beautiful world for us to relish. In long-run, IoT devices will be distributed with Blockchain at the core and network of IoT-Blockchain devices will transfigure enterprise solutions to a level not seen before. HTC Exodus is a one-off example that has seen the day of light already.

5. Larger Consortiums: Investors are now proactively seeking innovative ways of integrating this technology in new age as well as legacy solutions. Numerous players have partnered with blockchain technology providers, supported several research avenues and signed new consortiums. Hyperledger, R3 CEV, IBM, Ethereum Alliance, Bankchain and Oracle are some of the prominent consortiums. List is growing every day passing by and this is a great testament that technology has moved beyond hysteria and proof-of-concept phase.

6. Micropayments: Blockchain provides a exclusive prospect wherein all granular transactions can be done via wallet off-chain and tokens by means of micropayment channel. This will empower profitable models as blockchain propositions infinitesimal brokerage compared to Visa and MasterCard. Thorough transparency is maintained in blockchain providing trust among contributing entities. Over and above, blockchain is known for zero tolerance on security hence relevant for financial transactions.

7. Stable Coins: Cryptocurrencies are unpredictable hence not appropriate for financial alterations and acceptance. Solution lies in stable coins; which arose recently. Stable coins have steady prices and do not get affected by currency impulsiveness. This area of research and corresponding extension of regulatory framework will play crucial role in recognizing true potential of blockchain technology in finance sector.

8. **Interoperability**: Blockchain networks and DApps have grown exponentially. Blockchain interoperability objective is to expand information sharing across diverse networks and DApps. Industry will observe new technologies that enables blockchain interoperability. There are now few solutions such as Aion, BlockNet, Quilt, Phantasma, Polkadot and WanChain that are bridging the gap.

9. **Off-chain Components**: This is very important technology consideration and with a fully assimilated enterprise solution; off-chain is especially a key decision in blockchain architecture. Every information published to a stream can be on-chain or off-chain based on business necessity. There is need for on-chain processing in critical actions however there are numerous auxiliary actions that can be handled off-chain. Videos, images, libraries and large computing are appropriate candidates for off-chain consideration. On-chain and off-chain can be used within the same stream and various stream functions. This permits publishers to make the appropriate choice in a stream without compromising the speed. New age solutions will have substantial automation and autonomy that will take it to next stage of brilliance.

10. **Regulations and Tighter Control**: Numerous countries have stern regulations that administer blockchain platforms. In the coming time, speculations based cryptocurrencies bourgeoned everywhere will get truncated however genuine enterprise solutions will be endorsed by industry. Blockchain significance is beyond cryptocurrencies hence this will be a welcome news for technology advocates.

11. **Bio Crypto Economy**: Nano-robots ramble within human body to accomplish variety of health and economic improvements such as dynamic control of drug delivery, removal of cellular waste etc.

Trillion of cells with in humans necessitate coordinated automation for communication of nano-robots. Blockchain delivers granular communication coordination at enormous scale enabling logging, tracking, monitoring and consumption based pricing.

12. Fog Computing coupled with blockchain: This amalgamation will enhance performance to a level not seen before by partitioning application to run at the optimal network level. Blockchain will guarantee authentication of participants involved in computation and persist the transactions for better tracking & auditability.

Summary

Researchers around the globe have helped blockchain technology accomplish maturity and determination to meet industry and business expectations. Devices attuned with blockchain, micropayments, stable coins, advanced protocols supporting interoperability, high scalability and unification with AI and IOT will revolutionize industry in coming time. The proof of the pudding is in the eating. After years of hysteria, interest, pragmatism, reality-check and hands-on changes based on research and feedback, giant leap of blockchain into the future will see the day of light soon. We can see it coming. Do you?

As outreach of Blockchain becomes bigger in the coming years, smart contracts and Solidity will play pivotal role in benefiting entire world. Hope reading this book was an enriching experience to dear readers. Feel free to reach us with any queries or suggestions at below email address:

soliditybook@gmail.com

Wishing you best of luck in the word of Smart Contracts and Solidity.